The Apocalypse

The Apocalypse

David E. Müller

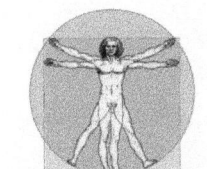

Vitruvian Publishing
2016

Copyright © 2016 by David E. Müller

All rights reserved. This book or any portion thereof may not be reproduced or used in any manner whatsoever without the express written permission of the publisher except for the use of brief quotations in a book review or scholarly journal.

First Printing: 2016

ISBN 978-0-9982629-0-1 (hardcover)

ISBN 978-0-9982629-1-8 (paperback)

Vitruvian Publishing
Warwick, New York

www.vitruvianpublishing.webs.com

Dedication

To my beloved family and friends for the continuous support and encouragment that a young writer greatly needed.
&
To my many teachers and professors that planted the love of literature and writing into my mind and spirit.

To each and all, thank you.

Table of Contents

Foreword ix
Act I 1
Act II 9
Act III 24
Act IV 37
Act V 72

Foreword

The notion of writing a tragedy that was a pastiche of Elizabethan drama had not arrived to me as an express intent; on the contrary it was rather a brief moment of inspiration that fuelled a desire for literary experimentation. Having completed the work almost a year's time from these words it seems most appropriate to consider the extensive effort and cultivation that was granted to the drama, and consequently provide material of interest for the reader that is curious of the work's history.

As I have made notice briefly already, the concept of writing a tragedy in the sort of English from the Elizabethan era (or rather, attempted), was an idea that was simply taken as an experiment to practise writing and comprehension of language. However, as with most curious cases, something that was hardly permitted much importance eventually grew to become a full-length, fully-developed drama. At the time that I penned the play to completion (as it is now), at age seventeen, I had already begun work on formulating the concept two years prior. Alas, youthful idleness had prevented any substantial progress on the work, and only when I had noted the potential in the play did the true effort begin.

I recall the reason that planted the desire to experiment in this form of drama being the reading of none other than William Shakespeare himself. Around my fifteenth year I had first read *Romeo & Juliet*, being struck by the wonderfully poetic nature of the work, but also by the allure of the archaic language. Furthering my reading in various writings from across the ages I found myself permanently enchanted by the literature of the classical, medieval, Renaissance, and Victorian authors. A profound sense of connection to these works and times was planted, and it would guide my style and character forever onward. Having already some experience with writing (but never in such a form), I was inspired; enticed to write in precisely the same language and style that had captivated me.

Thus, I began the first three scenes of what would later grow to become *The Apocalypse*. Initially, the story was relatively simple, yet resembled little of what it was ultimately to become. Again, I had not envisioned the drama to be given the effort it would, and indeed I had written so far as the third scene before I abandoned the work, having been too insecure and hesitant to toil on something I saw lacking in genuine literary quality. This mentality was soon subdued however, when I had further developed my writing abilities and was inspired with my readings of Shakespeare's *Macbeth* and Christopher Marlowe's *Doctor Faustus*. So I set once more to work and, in a little under an accumulated time of about a month, I had at last completed my drama, confident and exceptionally proud of my accomplishment. Certainly any boy of seventeen would be proud of having written ninety-six pages (in the original manuscript) of a pastiche drama that he had formulated entirely by himself.

Yet despite all the matters that had filled me with pride at the time of the play's completion, numerous shortcomings had become, and have become, apparent to me. Firstly, there is the mere character of the work. It had come to my mind on numerous occasions that there was the likely prospect that I would receive criticism for attempting to imitate the works of writers from the Elizabethan era, most notably Shakespeare. Truthfully, the purpose was never to imitate the genius of Shakespeare, but the inspiration from the Bard was profound. Realistically, no sensible person could assume that my mastery of the English tongue came (nor comes) even close to rival his, nor is my vocabulary ever likely to be something that can be compared. The appeal in writing *The Apocalypse* arose simply from the imagination and desires of a boy who adored drama in its archaic style (archaic in the sense of "Elizabethan" for this work) and from a love of writing in general.

However, a simple accusation of imitation is passable enough to ignore, though the matter of wording is perhaps of greater concern. In the ceaseless efforts to make the writing sound archaic, a great deal of understanding was likely sacrificed. On occasion there come parts of the play that perhaps sound rather confusing, yet a stubborn portion of my character abstained from revising such parts because of the spirit that was still infused in the line, and therefore the play. Furthermore, a comment that had been made numerous times by friends and family that had helped proofread the work was about the lack of stage directions and descriptions. This however, is not so much a shortcoming, considering the fact that the play is actually intended to be a closet drama to begin with, a work left for reading and not necessarily for performing (though it could by all means be performed), and the fact that I felt most of the imagery should be more expressed in the words of the characters.

With the previous considerations of Shakespeare and the other playwrights of his time however, there must be further examination of the poetic aspect in my own work of Elizabethan "imitation". While a great deal of poetry was infused within the dialogues and affairs of the drama, primarily in the slight symbolism and the creative metaphors utilised, still there was almost too little verse within the work to satisfy that condition. Despite the exhaustive attention I had given to maintaining a stanzaic form all throughout the play, the entire poetic nature of the work seemed to become faded, and fell into the background. The purpose of the drama had maintained its old character and story, yet had neglected the necessity of maintaining poetry in a piece so supposedly motivated by the works of Shakespeare or the Elizabethans.

Relating to the question of poetic quality, it will be evident to the reader the moment they begin the tragedy that there is the curious question of its form and organisation, and thus the subjects of its metre and order must be pondered. Most notably, there is the interest of the stanzaic structure that I had employed, and the question why it was at all added into the drama when there is no rhyme, and further, no metre to even qualify as blank verse at the least. Indeed, much of this decision lies within issues of ignorance, as I had not considered that Shakespeare's and Marlowe's dramas were not merely written in stanzaic forms out of convention, but for their employment of metred blank verse. Alas, I found this knowledge too late to change, and much of my patience would have worn thin to even contemplate changing the entire work to blank verse. In the end, we are left with a slightly poetic tragedy, which employs a stanzaic order without the addition of any verse or rhyme to supplement its poetic hint admirably.

Nevertheless, while the literature has its most evident shortcomings I could also be so bold to assure that some positive manifestations had occurred. One thing that was felt to have given the work an ounce of reality was the irrationality of many (if not all) of its characters. Regardless of the knowledge or ignorance that each character has of the philosophy and information that guides them, one after the other proves themselves to be irrational and foolish in their interactions or assumptions. A criticism that had been made in relation to this was how some of the characters could act so resolutely in their convictions when they had so little knowledge to their judgement. This was not a slight mistake of a novice writer however; it was, as a matter of fact, a very intentional addition. When one considers the nature of humans and their interactions, one cannot say that all they think or do is of a sensible temperament. Much as reality is not a convenient stream of logical ideals, I could likewise not form a pure arrangement of fantasy. This attempt at portraying the mentalities of man was perhaps one of the effective successes of the drama's writing.

Proceeding, it is my fervent hope that what was at least most apparent to all readers was the philosophical meditations that had evolved from both the subject material and the dialogue of the drama. The question of truth was perhaps the most monumental in the work, considering the sheer chaos that was manifested in the disputes of who possessed it. In slight relation to this was the fourth scene of Act Four, a philosophical (though fairly illogical) dialogue between the Librarian and Professor in regards to truth and prophecy. It was within this scene that the direct relationship to philosophy had occurred, not only from the Socratic dialogue, but also with the notable statement of the Librarian, "I know that I know nothing."

Beyond seemingly petty allusions to great philosophers, significant meditations of the philosophical sort most certainly were integrated into the very essence of the tragedy. One could undoubtedly devise trivial aphorisms from the tale, such as the likes of, "do not believe all that you hear", or "to have no friends is better than to have foul friends", but beyond these trifles it was my most genuine and deep desire to also discuss proper philosophy, perhaps in metaphysics and epistemology, but also in aspects that go in various other directions.

The esoteric and mystical interpretations are certainly evident where one looks. For example, in the first scene of Act Five the Librarian tells:

"Thy end may come in flood or fire all,
Man must learn that he is mortal,

And let so, oft seek the path of godhood."

This statement was intended to embody the mystical doctrine of transcendence that is so paramount to uphold in one's own mentality. Beyond this however, exist numerous other considerations into the question of prophets and the legitimacy of their claims. How may we assure ourselves that the words in our books, and from our prophets, are of truth? Where is it seen that words are written by man or by the divine? And how indeed can we seek to interpret the words of prophets when they may speak true words, but in poetry that has perhaps been read literally by others? The rest of the esoteric interpretations that could be made of my work I leave to the reader to seek and elect for themselves.

Political and (perhaps) martial principles evolved most profoundly with Lord Jakob's decisions and their successes or failures. Though he is frequent in his flaws, the occasions where the lord acts sensibly (intentionally written of course) allow for these concerns of state and war to evolve. Such a concern would be that one cannot allow their enemies to be seen as no threat from their small size, and indeed (though some may express disagreement) training troops in the art of subversion and spying is paramount where secrecy and covert organisations are concerned. In the execution of justice and the consolidation of auras of authority amongst the people, symbolic action may be necessary, though the circumstances for the deeds should be left for the ruler to decide with prudence and sensibility.

Nonetheless, whatever meditations *had* been formulated at the time of the work's writing (once more, merely a year before), there has still been a substantial shift in my personal philosophy from what it had been at the writing of the play to the state where I am now. I suppose this is as a consequence of youthful ambition and unfettered questioning that frequently includes one's own thoughts and philosophies. As I read through the work on numerous occasions to see what minute errors I may have failed to spy, there came the statements that I had stated that filled me with joy in having said, and the others that I looked upon with incredulity.

The concept of truth, and my assumption of its relativity, may seem clear to many when I considered the uncertainty of who possessed the true vision of reality in the work. I had seemingly stated often that truth lies within each man by different meaning or virtue, and therefore could be given no substantial and objective quality. I will not expound my complete philosophy on truth here, as that is best reserved for a more specific and bounteous essay in the future, but what should insofar be unmistakable is my rejection of this notion and my shift to what I can assume is my most solid philosophy. As the curiosity of truth was of the most significant role in the tragedy it was also the subject of most of my resentment, and beyond it there rested (thankfully) little else I could dispute.

To settle my mind with this commentary, and allow the reader to proceed with the reading of the drama, I will be brief in my concluding thoughts. It fills me still with great elation to know that I had successfully completed this work at so young an age, and regardless of what short-comings and mediocrity might be evident in this novice work, the experience was a process in learning, and whatever I may write hereafter shall have been built upon the wisdom that I received within this works creation. Now, to regard the creation itself I can only confess that in terms of emulating the historical works that offered inspiration, the tragedy is likely worth deeming a failure. Whether or not the story told commands attention, this I leave for the reader to conclude.

David E. Müller
September 2016

The Apocalypse

The Apocalypse
By David E. Müller

Dramatis personæ:
Harald, youngest son of Lord Jakob and brother to Andreas
Andreas, eldest son of Lord Jakob and brother to Harald
Vilagre, the leader of the cult
Lord Jakob, lord of the citadel, father to Andreas and Harald
Three Cultists, in brotherhood with Vilagre
Librarian
Captain, of guards in service to Lord Jakob
Professor, of the university
A Priest, of the temple
A Thief, to be punished
Two Guards, in service to Lord Jakob
Three Civilians, of the citadel
Advisor, in service to Lord Jakob

Setting: Citadel of Gevallenstad, in the Low Countries, at the time of the Renaissance.

Narrator
  Long in time hath man told tales of the world's end,
  Tales of prophecy left for man to contend.
  Here we are in Gevallenstad now placed,
  Set to spy two brothers, with these troubles faced.
  But what e'er shall these fates seek to bring to all,
  The fall of the beginning, or the beginning of the fall?

ACT I: Scene I
(Scene: A library with Harald, a book in hand)

                (Enter Andreas)

Andreas
  My dear brother, what dost thou read that makes thy eyes so tearful?

Harald
  O, dearest brother, I have upon mine eyes afallen,
  A most grave secret of horror and fatality.

The Apocalypse

Andreas
    What is that to affect thee with such sorrow?
    Crystals fall down thy cheeks round,
    As they do in the falls of mountains.

Harald
    How could a man not be so,
    When this tome tells of the end of our fair world?
    Life, as we know it to be in our eyes,
    All to end in sudden Armageddon.

Andreas
    In heaven's name, dear brother!
    Stand far from that tome,
    For it shall pierce thee with delusions,
    And visions of things not to come.

Harald
    Is there not an ounce of truth that lies,
    In these worn pages of old,
    Waiting to be found?

Andreas
              Far from it, say I.
    Those words that thou readest are written by madmen,
    That have had too much to drink,
    Or are effected by maladies of the mind,
    So to twist those, as foolish as thee,
    To drive themselves to horrid lengths.
    Come now to home,
    Rid thy mind of such ill thoughts.

Harald
    How can I? I shall not!
    E'en if it takes fore'er I shall stay here and find,
    If these tales speak true words.

Andreas
              Suit thy own will,

I have told thee my thoughts.
But speak not further ills to me,
Or of thy obscene tales,
For they do not grasp my attention.
Farewell!

(Exit Andreas)

Harald
Doth my brother speak truer words?
Have I come to insanity, been blinded by the ramblings of drunks?
I pray for my fate.

(Enter Vilagre)

Vilagre
I pray thou wilt believe when I say thou art not losing thy sanity.
What thou hast read speaks of tales and legends of old.

Harald
Who art thou?
What is thy business here?

Vilagre
I am hailed as Vilagre, and I come as the truth amongst lies.

Harald
What may thy duty be here within?
Speak fast, for thy presence is most unnerving at so late an hour.

Vilagre
I have seen that thy brother hath been blinded,
Blinded from the omen of fate,
But thou hast not. Pray thee, youthful one,
See that I come as thy saviour,
Thy prophetic kindred that thou shalt revere!
Wilt thou not hear my words?

Harald
Mayhap may my brother be true,

The Apocalypse

    Thou men that covet yon delusions hath quite the vile character.
    Thou art wizened and eerie, thy eyes are red as fire,
    As if under the influence of the herb.
    I want naught to do with thee!

Vilagre

    Foul, lying fool! Thou hast so spoken that thou believe,
    Now thou dost bring thyself to speak ill of my character?

Harald

    It shall stand that I shall hold with my brother to the end,
    Though troubles we may oft encounter.

Vilagre

    The end is surely nigh,
    It hath been spoken for hundred times before!
    Thou know'st of the secret, boy.
    To run from it, instead to halt its coming,
    Is most cowardly!

Harald

    If I believe of the end to come or not is not in question.
    I pledge fate to be challenged.

Vilagre

    The Revelation is near, child,
    Prepare for the fire to rain from the heavens!

Harald

    Speak thy horrid words no more, wretched man!
    I have no interest in thy ramblings.

Vilagre

    Leave at once! Leave thy new acquired wisdom and sink!
    Sink back to thy ignorant life of petty circumstance!

Harald

    So shall I do. I pray we meet no more,
    And when Death may come, I hope 'twill come for thee. Farewell!

Vilagre
>	Who are the weak but the simplest of sheep?
>	Minds so malleable for the strong to keep?
>	Where there rests e'en slight uncertainty,
>	Shall arise mayhap one who truth can see.
>	Fate gifts the patient, but alike the keen,
>	Who so act for their fortunes to convene!

(Exeunt)

ACT I: Scene II
(Scene: Night; a candle-lit feast hall where Andreas and Lord Jakob are seated at the table)

(Enter Harald)

Lord Jakob
>	My dear son Harald, what brings thee so late?
>	The feast lies begun, and thee we await.

Harald
>	Pray forgive my late entry, Father,
>	I was amongst the leaves of beauty and eternity.

Lord Jakob
>	Speakest thou of the library?

Andreas
>	Indeed, Father,
>	Where our Harald poisons his mind,
>	Alas, with the most wretched of writings,
>	That shall bring him to his self-harm.

Harald
>	Forgive my past tidings that angered thee so, brother.

Andreas
>	Hast thou given thy search to naught?
>	Praise heaven it be so!

The Apocalypse

Harald
    Nay, 'tis not thus,
    I shall delve e'er deeper in this curio of the globe.
    But alike, I will hold my tongue to speak not of it to thee.
    Nayless, withal, my belief hath wavered.

Lord Jakob
    'Tis a book that drives thee to each one's throats?
    Flushed with gall and wrathful fury thou art true!

Andreas
    Extend naught further in thy inquiry, Father.
    Mine brother, thy son, have we lost to madness and delusions.
    Forged by others of a likely temperament, nayless.

Lord Jakob
    Whye'er say'st thou he be mad?

Andreas
    Harald hath read a volume, wherein is told the end of all worlds.
    Such rot and vulgarity 'tis for me to speak aloud.

Harald
    'Tis my own conviction to be truth, Father.

Andreas
    And thus art thou a fool.

Lord Jakob
    Silence! Thy pesky bickering is alike that of birds!
    I bid thee good night,
    But speak not of these tidings with either or to I.
    Now go off to thy chambers, where to allay thy furies!

Harald
    (Aside) I need not stir to teach mine brother his blindness.
    Alas, his fate shall come at the end of time.

Andreas
    (Aside) Cursed, vexing fates,

Thou dost make my brother mad!
Yea, to extent that shall cause him naught but suffering,
In his course to halt that which he cannot grasp nor claim in truth!

(Exit Harald and Andreas)

Lord Jakob
    As two bold cocks fight for single hen,
    Where my sons are the fight, and truth, the hen.
    So proceeds the nature that is so well known,
    Now must we wait to see the yield of these seeds sown.
    As light in fog, is truth in men,
    As for both to slay the blesséd hen.
    Yet whate'er ills can be manifested here,
    Pray it does not spoil that we so earnestly endear.

(Exeunt)

ACT I: Scene III
(Scene: A dark grotto, with a fire pit betwixt its walls)

(Enter Vilagre and Three Cultists)

Vilagre
    Brothers three,
    I bid thee thanks for thy quick gathering in our sacred grotto.

First Cultist
    Think not of it.
    For what fate hast thou called?
    What hath itself revealed?

Vilagre
    I hail a hopeful new initiate into our ancient order of illumination.
    Though yet we need await his submission.

Second Cultist
    What his name?

Vilagre

The Apocalypse

                He hails to Harald.

Third Cultist
                The spring of Jakob?

Vilagre
    Aye, but with ill tiding extend I these tellings,
    For he hath another who doubts our revelation,
    That so evident to sane eyes.

First Cultist
    'Tis naught to make weary—

Vilagre
                          Nay, 'tis much in troubles.
    His brother, of whom I speak in another,
    Is as strong as stone in mind and soul,
    But he thinks naught to be plausible.
    His supports as sturdy as those of a tower or oak.
    But as a tree, he may be felled.

Second Cultist
    What course shall be taken?

Vilagre
    We shall use of his kin to corrupt his sense.

Third Cultist
    His brother? Our soon fellow, fate-willing?

Vilagre
    Aye, through false death or of rightful convert.
    For oft 'tis so from brother to brother, friend to friend,
    When one chooses, dual act.
    If not so, let us mould the mind of the boy alike clay,
    So to our whims he offers his.

First Cultist
    Would Harald slay his own kin?
    'Tis not chance he shalt feel guilt from the deed?

Vilagre
>	We shall make of him, with naught of weariness.
>	The nature of man in such a path is fair to play,
>	Tidings are clear, and thus, easy to convey.
>	For two men of single kind,
>	But share naught, for in different mind,
>	Shall slay to keep their word as true,
>	And stopper all that is marked as new.

(Exeunt)

ACT II: Scene I
(Scene: Harald, reading a volume in the gardens of Lord Jakob's keep)

(Enter Vilagre)

Harald
>	Guards, guards, intruder in the castle yards!
>	Make haste, mine life is in threat!

Vilagre
>	Silence thy tongue, foolish boy!
>	My desire is only to speak to thee as long as fates allow.
>	Pray give me a grain of thy term's sand.

Harald
>	Of what matter dost thou wish to squander the season?
>	Speak fast, or the steel of guards shall soon be upon thee.

Vilagre
>	Thou hast spoken thy mind most earnest, young lord,
>	Which I censured most brazenly.
>	For yet, in doing such an uncourtly deed,
>	I say I owe thee fair pardon.
>	Pray accept my foul speech as naught but vile,
>	Lay thy pardons on me.

Harald
>	Thou speakest most lavishly where thou canst plainly,

The Apocalypse

    Nayless, so shalt it be. Thou art pardoned.
    I fathom 'tis not only for this excuse that thou hast risked intrusion?

Vilagre
    Alas, 'tis indeed but one of reasons I come to thy walls.
    Yon secret, which thou and I have read, shall bind us.
    If thou dost allow it, my youth,
    I pledge to thee to join mine order of knowledge,
    And far-reaching clarity.
    Thus, thou art permitted learning of more,
    Within that tale thou hast glimpsed.
    Wilt thou accept my offer, O youngest, blessèd lord?

Harald
    What thou dost ask of me is no easy burden.
    My father, our Lord Jakob,
    Would not regard thy order in pleasant eye.
    Nor should mine brother, who abhors the mind of lofty mysticism.

Vilagre
    Gracious lord, most respectable prince,
    Such concern for thy kin's perspective is of most due reverence,
    But wouldst thou live thy life in shadows?
    Where all of concern are gone from the world?

Harald
    What speakest thou of?
    Thy speech is in riddles, and cloaks thy meanings in the dark.
    Speak clear, I pledge thee! Waste not my mind or my hours!

Vilagre
    Of thy time I shall not much more occupy, my lord.
    'Tis meant for me to say, that when the ends of times come to be,
    There shall be no kindred of thy blood to worry or to please thee.
    Take up the burden I shamefully give to thee,
    And follow the order that I plead to thee in grace.
    Broaden thy mind to stopper the game of gods,
    And live to see thy kith again!

Harald

Very well, mark my name,
And let my coming to thy order be known.
But note alike, I act so in amity to mine kin, not for self-lusting.
If so end our words, then I bid to thee farewell.

Vilagre

Many thanks to thee, my lord, and many blessings to thee.
There is yet one matter that I wish to ask still.

Harald

Have I not bestowed to thee enough of my existence?
What hast thou yet to say?

Vilagre

Thy brother—

Harald

                What of him?
What concern is he to thee?

Vilagre

Is he yet of stubborn mind? Yet of sceptic character?
Would he not wish to learn of the revelation,
To pledge alike to the brotherhood I spoke?

Harald

My choice is of my own, leave my kindred from thy worries.
Speak no further of my brother, leave him be.
Once more, I bid thee good night.

Vilagre

Indeed, indeed, my lord. Forgive my folly.
I shall make my leave.
When I call upon thy presence needed,
A note shall be given to thy guards.
But 'til those times, I will remain forgotten.
Farewell!

                                              (Exit Vilagre)

Harald
>   Would my father me forsake,
>   When I tell of the path I take?
>   Would my brother care for naught,
>   When the end brings the world to rot?
>   Time shall reveal to me,
>   Of what my life shall mould to be.

>   (Exeunt)

ACT II: Scene II
(Scene: The dark grotto of the order, where within sit the Three Cultists)

>   (Enter Vilagre)

Vilagre
>   Brothers of the flame, I call to thee!
>   Fair news I bring to tell of he!

First Cultist
>   What news so fair to alight thy orbs in joy?

Second Cultist
>   What news so fair to fill thy lungs with gasps?

Third Cultist
>   Speak quick, make haste, night is afoot.
>   Our turn has come, and deeds are to be done.

Vilagre
>   Brothers, the seed of Lord Jakob,
>   Empty and bending of mind is he so simple.
>   My sly words and sharp tongue have done their work,
>   And turned Harald to a brother of our order.

First Cultist
>   Much of joy is this!

Second Cultist
>   All to fall in plan!

The Apocalypse

Third Cultist
    Halt thy tongues and speech, brothers,
    The matter hath not been closed.
    What of his brother Andreas, eldest of Jakob,
    What news hast thou to tell of he?

Vilagre
    Still in foolish scepticism is he,
    But in time with his brother, our brother now as well,
    He shall for certain be in agreement. Nayless with little choice.

First Cultist
    Let us not fret with the tidings of fools,
    Those who mock and point to our order in jest.
    Lay 'pon us more news of Harald!

Second Cultist
    How was his reception?
    How was his conversion?

Third Cultist
    Indeed, what news doth yet remain in the affair?

Vilagre
    Guards most inept have they on watch.
    I, in bristles loud and thick,
    Could pass under the nose of the sentries,
    With nary a sight nor catch.
    There sat in the garden the young lord Harald,
    Unseeing was he, and startled great,
    When my presence was known to he.
    For the guards did he call, but ne'er did they come,
    For deep in sleep or filled with drink were they.
    First in anger did Harald fie me leave,
    But in my tone did he hold his tongue of rude displeasure.
    My pardons I gave, and begged from he,
    And foolishly did he them bestow.
    With time and plenty words, Harald did submit,
    Accepted my bidding, and hastened me to leave his keep.

The Apocalypse

First Cultist
    Foolish boy, stupid princeling.

Second Cultist
    Foolish, but to our use, a blessing.

Third Cultist
    So is it fair and of greater chance, verily,
    That our plans may in success be crowned.
    And now in joy we turn to Andreas,
    How shall we act to change his substance?

Vilagre
    If stubborn he still elects to remain,
    When his brother doth tell him of his choice and benefit,
    Then only horror befits his crime.
    We shall with Harald,
    Who so blindly follows as a sheep the bellwether,
    Mark the throat of his brother with steel.
    Then he shall halt our progress no more.

First Cultist
    But the matter still remains—

Second Cultist
    Would Harald commit so grievous a crime?
    To be fore'er marked a kin-slayer?

Third Cultist
    Be joyous if thou hast a plot therefor, Vilagre.

Vilagre
    So do I hold, keep patience and I shall tell.
    Harald is weak of mind, and a fearful youth.
    He knows not his way in the game of heaven,
    And is pleading for companions and acceptance,
    In the streets of the citadel.
    Both for his pleads of friendship,
    And with our clever ploys,

The Apocalypse

        We shall twist and contort his mind to our will.
        Our servant he shall be, though brothers he hails us as.
        Then, with time thou hast need to give me,
        Harald shall spill the blood of his brother,
        With naught a moment's halt.
        Leave thy concerns of him to be my burden.
        Thou, noble brothers, have played thy part so far well,
        And shall not toil soon.

First Cultist
        Well hast thou done, Vilagre, and honest hast thou been with us.
        In thy struggles thou shan't be one.
        We art here—

Second Cultist
                To be of aid to thee.
        Glory shall befall us,
        And saviours of pitiful, foolish man shall we be hailed.

Third Cultist
        "Hail, hail, hail the flame,"
        Shall ring through the streets of the citadel,
        "Our gods have come."

Vilagre
        Ere the fall of man and time shall we be strong.
        The order that is fathered here will call the fires back to their abyss,
        And thus live for an eternity.
        Brothers, the creed!

All
        When darkest times are filled to top with blood,
        And gods call upon the death of man by flood.
        Ascend shall a light to save the shadowed day,
        Where to be gods whilst old gods decay.
        New players shall arise to play fate's game,
        We are they, the Order of the Flame!

                                                  (Exeunt)

ACT II: Scene III
(Scene: The chambers of Prince Andreas, who sits atop the bed)

Andreas
    A knock at so late an hour,
    Haste and halt, who stands before my door?

Harald
    'Tis I, thy brother Harald.
    Youngest of the Lord Jakob.
    Messages have I fit for thy ears.

Andreas
    Enter—

                                           (Enter Harald)

Harald
    Pray forgive my late coming, brother—

Andreas
    Thou art forgiven. Close the door, I beg thee.
    The hour is late, and I fear to wake others in the keep.
    Now, pray tell what reason thou hast to come here.
    If thou wouldst talk of thy delusions, I wish to hear naught of them.

Harald
    Patience, brother, patience.
    'Tis not for thee, or the tidings of thy mind, that I intrude.
    'Tis for a matter of my concern, though thus also to plague thee.
    Pray anger not, and listen to the fullest.

Andreas
    Thy words evade their intention.
    Alike, they confuse and befuddle.
    Speak clear; what worries dost thou have,
    To plague I and thee, as thou hast so fearful claimed?
    Thou hast not done bloody duel once more,
    Nor wagered thy coin to naught?
    Naught to bear witness to father's wrath and shame?

The Apocalypse

Harald
    Nay, brother, 'tis not so.
    Alas, what I speak must regard my 'delusions', as thou hast put.
    But 'tis a matter that must worry me, if thou hast no objection.

Andreas
    Speak, I demand of thee, speak!
    Hold thy words back no longer!

Harald
    I have, by choice of none other but that of mine,
    Joined the brotherhood of an order,
    That which hath devoted itself to the study,
    And silent meditation, of the greater mystery.
    That of the world and its demise, which thou dost vehemently reject.

Andreas
    Thou fool! From whom didst thou hear of this order,
    This collection of sickened madmen,
    Who shall do naught but drive thee to madness thyself?
    Who is this serpent-tongued villain who pierces thy ears,
    And thus thy mind,
    With these obscene ravings?
    Who, I force thee, who?

Harald
    Tame thy rage, brother!
    Thou must watch thy words,
    For they are most unjust and of bitter insult.
    The man whom thou dost pay such abuse is called Vilagre—

Andreas
        Vilagre!
    A plenty name for such a vile character!
    A villain is he no less, I gamble with little doubt.

Harald
    Silence, I demand, thou goest too far!
    Who is this man to thee that thou must curse and ridicule his title?

The Apocalypse

Andreas
>Likewise, who is this man to thee, that thou,
>In protective and strong nature,
>Dost hold his name in such regard?

Harald
>Vilagre, this example of knowledge manifested with the age of time,
>Is but an elderly decrepit man.
>Of flesh, yea! But his mind,
>His mind, dear brother,
>Is of such excellence.

Andreas
>What wisdom doth he bequeath upon thee,
>So full and pregnant with poison of the soul,
>That thou dost trust him as thou wouldst a grandfather?

Harald
>Of that have I told plenty.
>His order, and he along,
>Are of the study of the mysteries of the world,
>And of its soon demise.

Andreas
>Spirits—spirits—spirits of rightful answer!
>Cycle, and cycle e'er more, thou parrot away.
>Once again of this ludicrous book,
>When thou speakest of 'mystery', nayless?

Harald
>So it is brother,
>But of this I wish none more to hear.

Andreas
>Where dost thou flee now?
>Halt, move no more,
>I shall go to our father,
>And tell to him of thy foolish election.
>Flee not from thy fate, as a coward does.

Harald
>Go to him, he shall be of no venom,
>As thou hast so cruelly spoken to I, thy kin.

Andreas
>So far have I held peace;
>No longer, say I!
>This inferno has met ends long too far,
>And thus I end its madness with whom power doth reside.

>>(Exit Andreas)

Harald
>Whither goest thou?
>Halt, Andreas! Halt, brother!
>I beseech thee!

>>(Exeunt)

ACT II: Scene IV
(Scene: A study, where Lord Jakob sits amongst deeds and papers at the desk)

>>(Enter Andreas and Harald)

Andreas
>Father mine,
>Where art thou?

Harald
>Andreas, hold thyself back.
>I implore thee, listen!

Andreas
>Lay not thy hands upon me, fool!

Lord Jakob
>Silence, my sons, silence I bid of thee.
>The keep lies asleep, and here thou,

Andreas
    With lungs out in holler,
    Wilt wake all who rest.
    What troubles thee to duel again?

Andreas
    Father, pray thee, trouble not to stand.
    Stay seated, and open thy ears to what I bring.

Lord Jakob
    So shall I do, my heir.

Andreas
    My lord, dost thou recall to fact the quarrel,
    Some time ago uncertain,
    Between my brother and I?

Lord Jakob
    Quarrel? The one at feast, not e'en four days hither?
    The one of rage and fateful philosophy?

Andreas
    The very same we have need to witness again.
    Alas, though one would let sleeping wyverns slumber,
    The beast has awoken and rears its vile likeness with much power.

Lord Jakob
    Troubles renewed, reborn in short time?

Andreas
    Indeed so, Father, and, most shamefully,
    Renewed to such lengths to worry thee.
    My brother Harald, thy youngest,
    Cherished by our tormented mother, thy earnest beloved—

Harald
        Brother, please,
    I beg of thee—

Lord Jakob
        Hold thy tongue, boy!

Continue in thy report, Andreas.

Andreas
    So shall I, Father, pray thee listen.
    Yea, the beast has awoken and comes to haunt our keep.
    My blood boils when the thought comes to grip my mind.
    Here he stands, now in sullen coyness—
    But ere this, in sovereign pride—Harald.
    He, though he knew of thy rage and retribution,
    And of mine alike unfeeling,
    Had elected, in much haste no doubt,
    To pledge himself in brotherhood to the 'Order of the Flame'.

Lord Jakob
    To what doth this vile name belong?

Andreas
    'Tis an allegiance that devotes itself,
    With raving and rabid madness,
    To the apocalypse they pledge to come.
    'Tis this that Harald hath sworn oath to,
    To both ideal and to order.
    He quoth that through it he shall gain wisdom,
    But to this say I he shall lose freedom.
    Thou know'st, dearest father, the tidings of these orders,
    Led by powerless madmen, lustful for dominance.
    Pregnant with lies of godly wisdom,
    And of saving in dire straits,
    But alas, shall do naught to bless their followers,
    And aught to hold their governance of minds.
    So has Harald, our dearest brother and son,
    Forsaken his kin, betrayed his blood,
    Forgotten his role, and abandoned his discernment.
    He hath so chosen, by no word but his,
    To enlist to this union of shadow,
    And thus leave us and leave his home,
    To devote himself to a false prophecy.
    So it is spoken, so did it occur, my Lord.

Lord Jakob

'Tis so true? So painful in re-utterance is it.
Do not forge a myth, a falsehood!
Thou hast so slandered thy name,
So humiliated us before the people,
And before the eyes of heaven.

Harald

Yea, Father, my brother speaks true words.
No words will I likely deliver that make amends;
But pray thee, wilt thou not be hearkening?
So is my suspicion, this prophecy foretold,
But wilt thou not bear open mind to my tales?
When man declares devotion to the heavens,
Is he so cursed as one who claims truth elsewhere?
In man, tome, or spirit?
Indeed, so do I claim belief, and,
If thou wouldst throw me from thy blood,
For such a trifle of conviction,
I shan't have further words with thee,
Who father claims to be.
Through only dusty tomes of ancient lore,
Delve I to seek the prophet's words.
'Tis not so fanciful and surreal a word,
That the world comes to its own end, as everyman.
Man passeth from life into death,
Shall not so the world do alike?
Nay, Father, thy harshest decree I cannot obey,
Let me live in how I see fate unfold,
And so shall I to thee repay.

Lord Jakob

Foul, foul fates upon me befallen!
Place not before me so insolent a man,
So prideful of his sacred word
That he denies his father's governance.
I, who in part placed him on this world,
Forsaken for some fanciful delusions.
I'll have it not—Nay,
How can I bear to have in life forgotten all of value,
To cherish a word so briefly in hold?

'Tis not belief that worries my wearied soul,
But allegiance to some shadowed men.
Consort of lunatics, concubine of lies,
Thou art naught but so a shell.
My flesh and blood, that I by word abuse,
Why hast thou driven me so far?
Alas, to be so far driven demands of me further requirements.
My son thou art—
Until time ends and the world burns beneath the heavens—
Yet no longer can thou reside in my hall,
Under my name, no longer.
I cast thee off, no son have I in thee.
Begone, away from my glistering eyes, begone.

Harald
Father, nay, make not such an election.
I beseech thee, in heaven's name,
Pray have a receiving mind,
To my beliefs grant acceptance.
Such a hasty destiny do not speak,
My voice can bear no further cries!

Lord Jakob
Nay, thou dost permit me no extended will.
So must life commence, so must we make peace.
Forsake thee I shall ne'er do,
But leave, thou must, as true as life.
I must ask thee now to go and fare well.
My sight cannot long last to spy thee in such a state.

Harald
Farewell, farewell, O Father, O brother.
Farewell to the keep, and be well to another.
Life has no further mystery,
Then can reside within its simplicity.
Where shall I walk, where shall I wander,
Now that I have been cast asunder?

(Exeunt)

ACT III: Scene I
(Scene: The dark grotto of the cult. Vilagre and Harald, now wearing the inky robes, wait)

Harald
>Dear Vilagre, what further praises can I on thee bestow?
>To take me when my need was greatest,
>Where for hearth I shivered,
>And for health I starved.

Vilagre
>My youngest, blesséd, Harald,
>When thou camst upon my grotto door,
>In that frosting fog of the night—
>Rare a cycle of the milky orb had passed, yea, I recall—
>How could I not take thee into the warming hold of my hospitality?
>Yea, as if thou werest my own I kept thee,
>And as if I was thy father, thou hadst put thy trust in me.

Harald
>Ere that holy day that I, most wisely so,
>Threw the cloak of familial identity from my shoulders, was I,
>With most sorrowful burden, in thy mercy.
>Thou couldst kick me from thy door, but did not so elect.
>Bless thy heart and soul!

Vilagre
>Thy praises are too much, my lord,
>And in shorter time may be uttered.
>Stay thy words for a moment's beat,
>For I shall soon foresee our brother's coming.

Harald
>So shall I silence my speech,
>O gracious brother.

Vilagre
>As if my word was prophecy,
>Here come our shadowed fellows three.

The Apocalypse

(Enter Three Cultists)

First Cultist
    So with us all assembled,
    May we begin our rite of meet.

All
    Ere foul kingdoms fall in flame,
    Ere the world falls in sullen shame,
    Shall arise an order of sovereign shine,
    To free the mind of caged confine.
    Fates befall thy sights on us,
    And mark our rite here to discuss!

Vilagre
    And now, brothers, may we commence.

First Cultist
    Yea, so shall we,
    What matters have we to regard, pray tell?

Second Cultist
    It doth concern thee, our brother Harald.
    What further news have thee of thy brother Andreas?

Third Cultist
    Hath he held adamant by thy loss?
    Hath he crumbled into vastness of ruin?

Harald
    Thou art my brothers only, O sacred four!
    No kinsman hail I by Andreas!

Vilagre
    Yea, so is all well, youngest,
    But couldst thou mark thy brother *past*?
    Thou knowest him well,
    Act not ignorant of his memory.
    In good spirits, e'en if hatred boils,
    Tell our brothers three what news hath come to thee!

The Apocalypse

Harald
    Yea, so shall I accept thy words.
    No news bear I of Andreas,
    Cursed may he be, and my naming tongue!
    My former father Jakob, no lord can I title him,
    Hath called for the finding of our order, as I hear often well.
    Fear not, fret little, foolish hath he been.
    Overground, through the citadel, and heaven above,
    Doth he look violently with rage,
    But he knows not where we lurk.
    Here, in the womb of the earthly mother.
    Andreas hath kept within the keep,
    Or so hath his father decreed,
    In fear of losing but another of his seed,
    To the hands of the truth he so abhors!
    Nayless, so may we commence if thou seest it fair.

Vilagre
    What plans make thee of this, my brothers?

First Cultist
    Find we wise yet to proceed with he?

Second Cultist
    Andreas may arm our order strong,
    To destroy the soul so ruined of the Lord Jakob.

Third Cultist
    Yea, so have I the plan of victory!
    Mark brothers, hear my words,
    And follow with fellow theory if so needed.
    Mark we Harald, loyal to us throughout,
    And loyal unto death no doubt.
    His falling from his father's might,
    Hath weakened the soul of the Lord Jakob.
    Herewith take we Andreas, by death or by life,
    By heart or by knife, and further go so on.
    Have we Jakob lose e'er more the citadel shall fall in chaos.
    The people shall thirst for blood of the lord so inept of heart.

The Apocalypse

      Anon shall we act as great lights for those so fearful,
      Of the future and of their lives,
      And so shall the Apocalypse be quelled!

Vilagre
      Yea, but what shall we do ere the fall?

First Cultist
           What of Andreas?

Second Cultist
           How shall he turn?

Harald
      Hush, brothers, pray thy ears agape!
      Well know I this stubborn oak's ailings,
      And greater know I his vexes.
      Turn he shan't, save with truthful threat.
      Fear not, for I do not, the spilled blood of my elder brother.
      The blood that runs within my veins,
      Is not the same that runs in Andreas';
      For 'tis the soul that makes men brothers,
      As blood is passed but in common lineage.
      If e'er there was a time to act,
      Mark we now, quick as hares, sly as snakes,
      To strike the lord's son and end the strife.
      Let the time of the flame be lit,
      And blood of the unworthy be spilt!

Third Cultist
      Loyal brother Harald,
      So spoken as e'er the brightened herald!
      Temper though, much as it is of need,
      Thy raging hate and anger.
      A closing tie may we seek to call Andreas' faith,
      Into the grasps of our order holy.
      Remains he stern and oakish as the cosmic pillar,
      Then time for blood hath come early.
      So pray, brothers, here lies our plan!
      Ere the twilight ring at dusk has rung,

The Apocalypse

> And all but few remain in sleep,
> Go we to the keep's walls,
> Fro the garden so open to all and sundry,
> And let fair Harald go forth to speak.
> May Harald speak to his brother former,
> To which Vilagre may come to shield our's.
> Yea, and if Harald shan't see his deed done,
> And Andreas, as stern as stone still remains,
> Mocks and curses our order further,
> Arise we three from brush and bush.
> With holy intent, and fateful steel,
> Make we active the web of time.
> Andreas shall falter and perish then,
> And Jakob will fall on faulted melancholy.

First Cultist
> And so shall we reign—

Second Cultist
>   Yea, after so long a time, at last—

Third Cultist
> Pray it to be so brothers,
> Let fate smile upon us.

Harald
> Let fate smile upon us,
> But let us know our deed.
> Let us act out of right,
> And upon our knowing.
> Haste, haste, I starve to act!
> Too long a time have I waited,
> But alike know I to plan well throughout,
> So thus no fault does us befall.

Vilagre
> And make thee well known to it, young one.
> With the blood of Lord's last son,
> Comes the light of the final dawn.
> Mark, thou fools with loyal hearts,

The Apocalypse

      As from the dark come a thousand darts.
      Hail and hail, and hail to we,
      Our time hath come, and kings we be!

                                                         (Exeunt)

ACT III: Scene II
(Scene: Night; Andreas walks amongst the keep's gardens with the Captain of the Guard)

Andreas
      'Tis an eerie night, wouldst thou not say alike, Captain?

Captain
      So would I agree in full, my young lord,
      But no reason less to fret with worry.

Andreas
      Yea, so would I commend agreement.
      But pray thee tell, Captain, and be true to me,
      Has naught thy eye and watch befallen?

Captain
      Nay, my lord. Not a soul nor a spectre have we spied,
      And pray it so remains.
      As thy father sits in melancholic weeping,
      The guard has eke shrunk in might.
      Hope that no madman may enter the keep in such ease.

Andreas
      Aye—O my poorest and grief-stricken father,
      What weakness have we withheld so long,
      And given to our youngest?
      Why hath my father brought from heaven such a fate, Captain?

Captain
      Alas, my lord, I hold not all-knowing.
      Heaven hath its ways, and no man can know of all its doings.
      Naught the sages do could grant them eternal clarity.
      Nayless, 'tis not fate that so plagues a man,

The Apocalypse

    Rather his weakness permits foulness to come.
    Yea, the hour is late my lord, the bells chime once,
    An e'er forbearing ring no less.
    I must set the guard, and myself my head then lay.
    So good night and fair sleep,
    Let not foul dreams awake thou keep.

Andreas
    Good slumber, night, and peace. Farewell!
    Ere morning's shine I shall no doubt lay here as well;
    Sleep having taken me,
    And light, no power to awaken me from deepest spell.
    No matter—Sleep, good friend, and sleep thee well!

                                        (Exit Captain)

    And so I forsooth to be lonely as the moon,
    That awaits her own fall while the rest await the sun.
    So shunned by man, and by heaven twice alike,
    But e'er so bright as nature may make her.
    And of what nature can we talk of this solitary soul,
    That so humbly strolls amongst the shadowed green?
    Is his heart so cloaked as yonder water black,
    Is his soul so rigid as yonder oak erect?
    Or is he so bright and weak as the sun-loved flower,
    Abloom and alight amongst the rich grasses?
    Is he fair a son but foul a brother,
    Or foul to family and fair to the mass?
    Is he worthy to fall heir to his father's crown,
    Or only fit to stroll the streets a beggar?
    So question, so question, each man his worth,
    Ere he think himself vilely virtuous.
    So proud had I stood to be loved by my father,
    And to do all justice for our family against my brother.
    But so guilt-pierced am I still that I have cast out my kin,
    Since birth to await and since birth to love,
    Now with not a moment's thought,
    With naught a glory's glare, have I lost a light of life.
    And so I go on—
                Halt! Who walks in yonder shadow? Speak!

The Apocalypse

(Enter Harald)

Harald
    Greetings to thee, Andreas.

Andreas
    Thou! Thou so wicked to show thy face here,
    But whose likeness I am so joyous to see e'er again.
    Why comest thou here? What foolishness hast thou done?
    Art thou now free again of mindful bonds?
    Hark! Make well not to be spied by our father.
    O brother! Well have thou gifted me!
    Hast thou not come to make amends at last?
        Halt, what see I here?—
    Nay, thou foul braggart,
    Curser of names, smearer of virtue.
    Here dost thou stroll, as if a maggot crawling to warmth,
    Bearing those damnable robes of Moorish black,
    Of such offense to our father so irked by dejection.
    Fie, and fly from this place whence thou hast been cast aside,
    Thy lechery of the soul is of no mercy here!
    Speak, villain, speak! Why dost thou walk amongst the shadows?

Harald
    I see thy stubbornness hath not allayed itself, Andreas.
    Nor hath thy string of slander itself soothed.

Andreas
    Why dost thou hail me by my common name,
    And not by affectionate title?
    Am I no brother to thee any longer?

Harald
    I have but few brothers now at times,
    In a count of four, not having thee.
    Too great hast thou wronged and cast me,
    But I have a greater purpose here to serve.
    I come to thee, Andreas, as graciously as e'er,
    In a final movement of grateful gesture.

Wilt thou not bear my words?

Andreas
    I predict thy message well already,
    But out of the ounce of love I have left for thee,
    I will leave thee to speak.
    But do so in haste, my anger rises e'ermore,
    As the souls rise to the heavens upon their mortal death.

Harald
    Thou, O former brother mine,
    Hast spoken oft, and harsh as fire, of thy disdain for my order.
    The one thou seest so vile and shaken to a corrupted core.
    But hark! I stand before thee a new man,
    So nigh to greater immortal attainment,
    That mortals could not fathom.
    I have been nursed to health and greater strength,
    Since our gracious father threw me from his keep,
    This keep thou liest in luxury here within.
    Dost thou recall that day so good and well?
    Dost thou recall e'er well along, Andreas,
    Of the foolishness thou hadst so spied in truth?
    The book thou hadst seen as falsehood and farce,
    Without a moment's glance within?
    From ignorance spoke thou as one well read in that tome's words,
    And such is irrational foolishness.
    Dost thou recall Andreas, thy betrayal to me so willing,
    To our father Jakob who thou knowest was so devoted to his pride,
    Whose reaction was so commanded by self-image?
    But nay, I am not here on vengeful desires,
    I am here for duty of conversion.
    For a second's beat, younger lord, elder mine,
    Canst thou not see the value in this order?
    Canst thou not see the knowledge in its grasp,
    The brotherhood it shall give?

Andreas
    Thou speakest of duty but bring up ills to thee.
    Thou speakest of value but bring up foolery.
    Thou speakest of brotherhood but speak not of friends once got.

The Apocalypse

        Thou hast sought knowledge, but thou hast found naught!
        The youth is so clear in thy words,
        No understanding, no thought,
        Hast thou given to the matters I had brought,
        And to the words our father uttered on thy falling from the kindred.
        Thou hast spoken of friendship, and family, and knowledge all,
        Hast thou forgotten so soon of what thou once hadst?
        Hast thou known clarity in those times, e'er less than now?
        What man art thou to grovel to men thou dost not know?
        This order, this cult of thine, I want naught to do with.
        Be gone, be gone, and think what thou hast done.
        Mark only thy mind, severed from reason,
        But also thy kin from that heart of thine!

                                                        (Enter Vilagre)

Vilagre
        Still stern as the ox and stubborn as the dam,
        Art thou not, Andreas, eldest of Jakob?

Andreas
        No surprise can I feel to see my brother's puppet-master,
        Who so slightly pulls and plucks the strings.
        Was it thy desire for he to come to me?
        To try e'ermore and grasp my wilful sense to thy cult?

Vilagre
        Temper, temper, younger lord,
        Think not we work alone.
        For where there are great ideas, come great men.
        Where great men lurk come great masses,
        And therefrom comes the rise of empires.
        But listen e'er once more,
        I extend the hand of gratitude, the bidding of fraternity.
        Dost thou not desire have to reconcile with thy brother?
        Dost thy curiosity not itch to know 'the else'?
        Wilt thou not give us thy purest thoughts, ne'er once?

Andreas
        Give me but once glance into thy eyes,

The Apocalypse

       So glazed and lost within their one gaze.
       Give me but one glance to my brother,
       So given and lone to thy words,
       And I know there is no mystery to thy intent.
       My brother is used, as alike art thou;
       I grant thou art no order-leader, villain,
       For leaders cannot be alike to thee.
       They must know to be wrong, to be prudent in all forms,
       But naught of the sort dost thou portray!
       Wisdom I shall myself seek, to know what I perceive;
       Not to be told the meaning of some book,
       Which I couldst read as divine messages from the veil.
       So hang thy order, and let it burn,
       I pray heaven will save thee from thyself!
       No kings shalt thou be, yea I know thy plans,
       For no folk would be so massively lost to bear thy rule.
       Thou art the downfallen victims, no greater wilt thou be,
       By all the divines, I command fate upon to thee!

Vilagre
       And so end the tidings of the destitute,
       Thy end has all but known its end.
       Brothers, from the shadows, arise!

                            (Enter First, Second, and Third Cultist)

Andreas
       See how I admit my wrongs!
       Thou hast more than thy dual foolish.
       But mark also, I have not changed my philosophy.

First Cultist
       To thee we grin—

Second Cultist
             With shock and gladness in—

Third Cultist
                 To know our time can begin.

The Apocalypse

Harald
    O brother Andreas,
    Why couldst thou not see what fate could fairly thee befall?
    From side to side we could stand.

Andreas
    I would have favoured to stand with thee in the light.

Vilagre
    Andreas, prince as heir, eldest of Jakob, who is lord of the citadel,
    I beseech thee one final time longer!
    Wilt thou not join us in rank to rule?
    Wilt thou not join us in order to seek?

Andreas
    I would rather ne'er rule, than rule a tyrant free.
    I would rather ignorant be, than be a slave to thee.

First Cultist
    So hath he spoken—

Second Cultist
        So hath he decreed—

Third Cultist
            So hath he sealed his fate.

Vilagre
    And see, so do the times proceed.
    Alas, 'tis a shame our brother Harald must stand alone,
    But fates alight he hath us as fairer oath-brothers.

Andreas
    Fool! Blood is the bond that binds men!
    From Briton to Briton, Teuton to Teuton,
    Latin to Latin, oath hath but different value.
    'Tis the blood that keeps these folk alive;
    Strike it dumb and into sand they fade.
    Thou hast revealed thy ignorance clear,
    Now seest thou what I mean, brother?

The Apocalypse

      Knowledge hath he mayhap in that book, but naught in all else.
      As foolish as thou and I, men are we,
      And men be foolish, but we need not be dumbed!
      Foolish is everyman, ignorant as well,
      But wielding our souls, 'tis the greatest aid of all.
      To know some is as well as to know all!

Vilagre
      Enough banter, the time for speech is at its end,
      For action hath come at last. Brothers in place!

Andreas
      Mark thee, hear my words for eternity!
      Whate'er thou mayst wreak upon me,
      Shall my father, thy lord, grant a hundredfold to thee!

Vilagre
      We have no lords but ourselves—

First Cultist
      From blade to flesh—

Second Cultist
            From blood to blood—

Third Cultist
                  From bone to bone—

Harald
                      Shall rise our throne.

Andreas
      Guards, guards; in heaven's name arrive!
      Blood shall flow and I shall fall.
      Swords unsheathe and justice serve,
      Ere the time too late hath come.

Vilagre
      None can hear thee, young prince,
      They have all but gone to night's bidding.

Harald
> Farewell, Andreas, brother once.

> > > (Andreas dies)

Vilagre
> And so hath it ended,
> So may we continue.

First Cultist
> Now, brothers, may we proceed,
> Our time hath come, yea, blessed befallen.

Vilagre
> So as blood runs red, alike the set of sun,
> An era ends and the deed lies done.
> The realm shall fall and the people fear,
> But we now rise to protect their dear.
> The lord is lost and hangs his head in shame,
> So doth command the Order of the Flame!

> > > (Exeunt)

ACT IV: Scene I
(Scene: The library, where the Librarian sorts his tomes in silence)

Librarian
> Books of new and books of old,
> From the lowest low and highest reaches.
> Organised on present day and on yester-day,
> Yea, so e'en the day of the yester-day throughout.
> What drudgery I do so regard with love and passion,
> Alike with much resentment,
> When my twice placed feet land the bedside floor.
> Mark! This tome of exquisite leathers and markings,
> And mark, another! So illuminated with sun-lit gold.
> O, but this one of naught special,
> So bland and of low quality,
> Rarer of words, and dull of thought—

The Apocalypse

How gracious I adore it indeed!
Alas, a visitor comes, and so privacy stalls for the given moments.

(Enter Harald)

Harald
Good health, book-keeper, fare thee well?
I come to seek the book.

Librarian
O, good sir, what book may that be?
Mayhap 'tis this one atop the table?
Or another aloft the chandelier?
Or moreover all the hundreds I have in stack?
Ne'erless, I grant I have thy "book of no name"; to give it one?

Harald
(Aside) Curse this senile old hobbler, too blind to work well.
Thou knowst which one, tome-holder,
The only one amongst any ready in worth.
What other tomes can offer more to man?

Librarian
I am not all-knowing, my good sir.
I may have amongst me so many volumes,
But I needn't have gazed within them all, though so I have.
Odd thought it seems,
I know still not which tome thou speakest with such endearment.
'Tis most certainly one I must have known,
But some aid might it be to have still its hail-mark.

Harald
O, inferno's fire, I shall seek it enough alone!

Librarian
Beware to search what we cannot e'en name, young sir.
E'er a befuddling task I bid thee it well to be.

Harald
Lo, so have I spied it, and so granted with no aid of thine!

The Apocalypse

Librarian
>No curiosities see I there, young sir.
>Markless, call I that tome,
>But for reasons twain.
>One, for the title it doth not bear,
>And two, for the little clarity it doth give to its reader.
>Words thrown in jumble, and with fogged meaning no less.
>But panic enough to give, I grant.

Harald
>(Aside) Naught but in riddles does this elder speak, alas.
>Nay, carest thou to refute thy claim,
>Or so to shield with logic?

Librarian
>Nay, I say neither. Patience have I little, and find squabbles petty.
>I am no philosopher or master of logic,
>I know only what I feel, and e'en of that am I not certain.
>'Sblood, I am but a book-keeper, boy.
>What more dost thou await?
>Read thy tome and fare thee well,
>More service can I not offer.

Harald
>Dost thou adopt indifference to feign thy strength?
>Or art thou ignorant, but dost not so profess?

Librarian
>Yea, apathy have I, for so to speak,
>And I must confess I am ignorant great,
>Of that which I do not know.
>But mark thee well, boy, disrespect shall be like repaid,
>To which I shan't hold objection.
>Foolishness may I bear,
>But harshness—not!

Harald
>Aye, erewhile I spoke to rash,
>And so crave thy pardon.

But of curiosity must I plead some more.
Thou hast read the book, as so self-told,
But what hast thou read betwixt the lines?
What message spied thee there, pray tell?

Librarian
    Of this can I not speak,
My word is but my own, and I know no prophecy.
What thou readst is what thou seest,
No word of man may change that.
I am no tyrant to teach thy mind in mine order,
What thou seekest is what thou must find thyself.
Only so canst thou claim sight within the world.

Harald
    Yea, so I see and shall seek anon in solitude.
Thus I take my leave, book-keeper.
Thanks to thy wisdom, toast I.
Good day and fare-well,
(Aside) For naught hast thou aided in.

Librarian
    Yea, so bid I thee alike!

                                                (Exit Harald)

So praiseful and sound did the boy speak,
Though once so venomous and harsh did he eke.
Great weakness sense I within his soul,
E'er the mark of a shield not whole.
I can profess a glimpse of what's to come,
A tale most sorrowed and e'er gruesome.

                                                      (Exeunt)

ACT IV: Scene II
(Scene: The chambers of the Lord Jakob, where the lord is in anguish upon the bed)

Lord Jakob

The Apocalypse

A son befallen to manic order,
Another betrothed to heaven's realm,
And so stand I, lone as a drifting leaf.
My only consolation to know that still one of my seed,
Though lost may he be,
Stays in sound life, vibrant and grim.
Weak-willed am I, to not grasp my senses,
And keep my sons close ere we were torn apart.
Andreas, my eldest Andreas,
Why didst thou have to die?
Did heaven mark thee too wicked for life?
Or, as I pledge, too pure for this muddled world?
Harald, my foolish son, though great love have I for thee,
Let not the rumours speak true words,
When they speak that thou hast had part in thy brother's death.
Couldst I still love a soul so wicked to slay a brother?
Couldst I still love a mind so pulled astray?
Alack! Fierce is my sorrow and great my pain,
But not so great as mine hate for me!
Sweet darling, where art thou still?
Dost thou not know thy children are lost?
Leave me in peace, come not to my room,
No lord can I stand to remain hereforth!
Hark and listen, a knock comes on my door,
State thy name and state thy challenge.
Speak well or leave me to be,
In softest, e'er torturous solitude to weep!

(Enter Servant)

Servant
    My lord, I heard thy tortured words,
    Much misery did they pierce within me—

Lord Jakob
                              Ho!
    Hast thou listened through my door?

Servant
    Only to hear what man could hear without need to spy.

The Apocalypse

      But pledge, my lord, no harm do I seek to do.
      I come only as a loving subject.
      A servant to a lord, a son to a father alike I see,
      Thy welfare is my duty, and for merriness do I serve well.

Lord Jakob
      Thy words are grand and full of love,
      But no malevolent trying of my tempers do I feel.
      Thou wouldst know my sorrow then,
      If thou hast heard insofar.
      Sons bygone to madness and mortem,
      And yet I still live to tell of their fates.

Servant
      Yea, my lord, so far have I heard, and so I came,
      Come to tell thee of a blessing sent from heaven;
      A notice from thy late elder Andreas!
      Yea, for I see it that he his fate had seen,
      And wrote for guidance to thee, if fate had so followed.

Lord Jakob
      Alike a message from beyond the burial,
      Blesséd fates both cursing and gifting.
      Haste! Let me spy this letter,
      So that I may hear the words of my son anew!

Servant
      Hidden below where his head did rest in sleep,
      Found we e'er the smallest note to be of length.
      To thee I give it, to hold to heart well on.
      Pray thee read it aloud, for much love had I for Andreas.
      Kindest was he to me, alike as thou art,
      What can he tell us from his prophecy?

Lord Jakob
      So hath my son written:
      "O, father mine, and lord of all us in the citadel,
      Dead foretell I to be when thou readest my words,
      For my stand against my brother's order new,
      Shall for certain enemies make.

The Apocalypse

Lo, do not thou lose hope, for I justice still seek,
E'en I lurk in realms hereafter.
My father, dear I love thee,
And for thee have respect unwavering.
But thou hast been foolish in thy search for the Order of the Flame.
That wretched brotherhood of lies and evil,
Who in truth seek not a greater mind,
But purely to gain thy crown of power.
Thy son Harald, my youngest brother,
Is but a pawn in their greater scheme.
He hath knowledge sought, yet did naught but lose his self-rule.
I must confess, though painful I find it to,
That Harald will per chance have role to play,
If my end comes to greet me anon.
And now to search for the Order,
And not to let them their goals attest,
Thou must act with haste,
But hark my words to favour me once more.
Dear father, thou hast spied in every hall,
In every street—yea, every land thou knowst.
But hast thou not thought to search the earth?
For where there is rock, and mud, and soil,
Thou shalt find rats and worms bountiful.
Mine prediction hath been stated,
But 'tis thy place to put an end to madness,
That hath so gripped our fair citadel.
Mark thee well, I sit in watch,
Upon the clouds of the firmament.
Let nature nurture and wisdom thou give,
To bring order to thy people.
Keep watch on who thou hast in company,
And, fair father mine, save thy folk and recall,
Beware the sleepers who lay awake."
O, dumbed perception, O cursed mind,
I bid I were hid out of sight!
Such shame and foolish humiliation have I,
For e'en the dead have better eyes than I.
Eldest son, heaven bless thee!
Thy memory shall stand hereforth,
As anger hath misplaced my sorrow.

The Apocalypse

        This order shall be stopped, I pledge.
        So bid I, fair servant, go forth,
        Rally our guardsmen and begin the search in earth!

Servant
        Yea, my lord, bless thy rage and honoured spirit,
        No shame shouldst thou feel.
        All men are once foolish,
        But the unwise have not intuition.
        Act, spoke Andreas, and to act thou didsr choose.
        'Tis not foolishness in my eyes!
        Hail to Jakob, lord of the citadel!
        Awake, brave men of the guard,
        The time for shadows hath come upon us!

                                          (Exit Servant)

Lord Jakob
        And so begins a war of thoughts,
        Long begun but little fought.
        One son taken as a traitor,
        Another slain for rightful spirit.
        No more shall I have of it!
        Here begins an era of hope,
        A time of righteous lordship,
        And of noble folk to live!
        No more shall I cower,
        No more shall I weep,
        No more shall I fail to sow the seeds I reap.
        Heaven give me the strength I need,
        And judgement I may not have.
        Jakob, lord thou art, but not so acted,
        And thus hast thou evil attracted.
        Go forth and conquer thy ground anew,
        Give the secret tyrants their just due.
        Victory, victory, for the dead and living,
        Remember their lives and be forgiving!

                                                (Exeunt)

The Apocalypse

ACT IV: Scene III
(Scene: The Guardhouse, where the Captain sharpens blades)

(Enter Lord Jakob)

Lord Jakob
    Captain! At attention, yet at ease.

Captain
    My lord, what brings thy majesty to here,
    Our musty quarters unfit for thee?

Lord Jakob
    My strong and honourable, ally.
    I have been most lost in use of my mind.
    Thou shalt have heard unto now,
    Of my eldest son's cruel murder in my dominion?

Captain
    Aye, my lord, and much does it ail me.
    Ere no more a minute's passing had I spoken to him in person.
    Alas, I had then left to form the guard,
    But too hindered was I to act in time.
    May his memory live in all our sorrowed hearts eternal.
    But what else can I aid thee in my lord?
    Having cost thee a son, in a manner,
    That much shame it doth me accost.

Lord Jakob
    Blame not thyself for what was my own fault.
    I, as his father, should have spied his movements clear,
    Having lost one son to other torture at the time as well.
    Nay, but I come to thee for it is time for action.
    I have remained still too long,
    And now have lost one son to death and another to himself.
    I cannot wait longer, for I know the two share link.
    We must use the guard to spy out the rats,
    Those that seek my downfall and the kingdom's ruin,
    And restore orderly sanity to the citadel's domain.
    Thou must call upon thy guards, and thy bravest men,

The Apocalypse

        To face the shadow of the unknown.
        I know not what force and blade these orders wield,
        And for all their deviance I must remain prepared.
        Thus I bid thee, wilt thou act with me?
        Wilt thou call upon our men, with which to search?

Captain
        My lord, think thou that this is wise—

Lord Jakob
                                  Aye,
        I have been so counselled already.
        I give my Advisor presence.

                                  (Enter Advisor)

Advisor
        Captain.

Captain
        Thy guide-ship—

Lord Jakob
        If thou seest fault in my plan, speak freely, Captain.
        We can certainly then denote our paths anon.

Captain
        My lord, pray thee well, what knowst thou of this order?
        Hast thou heard but rumours of their action,
        Or are they, as thou sayst, purely mad men?

Lord Jakob
        My captain, pray thee hear, my own son Andreas,
        Ere his early fate, had done his study well.
        He had known his brother's mind and kept close watch.
        He spied the intentions of this order,
        And all its wanton revelry.
        I know now that it is true,
        I know where they lurk.
        And if it is but a theory,

The Apocalypse

    It shall soon reveal itself to me.
    But in all cases some action in necessary,
    And if my council so agrees,
    Action shall be taken.

Advisor
    But wouldst thou risk the use of thy men for power, my lord?
    Then is great deal of time and gold expended,
    To order the guard as thou wouldst decree.
    It would be foolishness to take men from other issues,
    To fuel the aid of this vice.

Lord Jakob
    But wouldst thou risk the threat of revolution,
    For in investigation to be ignorant?
    Wouldst we not stand in shame,
    When our kingdom lies in other hands,
    Bidding we should have acted to turn fate?

Captain
    A fair remark, my lord, but an issue doth remain.
    What couldst we train the men in to aid this task?
    We know not what for to look, or for how great in number.
    We fight a war against mists and smoke.
    Whither do these worms lurk, as thou hadst spoken?

Lord Jakob
    O faithless friends, think so logically.
    I had done more minor a duty,
    But only with o'er-ground searches and minor numbers.
    Think thus; had I but a troop of five,
    And looked to the hall when they were in the tavern,
    And looked in the tavern when they were in the foundry,
    What endless chase is this?
    Note then also, I had only looked above ground,
    But not did I think in cave or grotto to search.

Advisor
    Absurd deduction—

The Apocalypse

Captain
    Impossible, my lord. How could an order so great a threat,
    Be stuck within the Earth as so?

Lord Jakob
    Mayhap 'tis not so great a number we profess.
    For with a smaller number concealment is but a simpler task,
    And unity arises e'er closer amongst groups small.
    As with a mouse and a bear,
    Thou canst hear the greater blunder,
    But the other not oft hear scuttle.

Captain
    So what dost thou elect us to do, O lord?
    Shall we take great number of the guard,
    Present them training in the art of spying,
    And so seek out an order unknown?

Advisor
    Shall we deprive the city of its protection?
    Shall we give them practise in the coward's art?
    Shall we search for what we do not know in place?

Lord Jakob
    Did my son merely disappear for joy?
    Did he desire merely to seek other home?
    There is no question of this order's presence,
    Though I shall confess I do not know its place.
    For that we seek it further.
    With that which we do not know, we must employ the art of spying.
    'Tis with silence and e'er presence,
    Not with thunders and vast armies, that this order we shall find.
    With ruinous intentions doth my throne face threat,
    And coward would I be to let it fall.
    But 'tis not so longer, for change is done anon!

Captain
    I shall go to foretell the guard their duty.
    So dost thy Will decree, my lord.

The Apocalypse

                                                                 (Exit Captain)

Advisor
    My lord, much honour do I seek for thee,
    And able know I thy fatherly duties.
    But dost thou truly think this action wise?

Lord Jakob
    Let not my disfavour come to thee,
    Action is taken, and 'tis but time for justice.
    Give me peace, retreat to thy chambers.
    Yonder day to come, we act at sun's rise.

Advisor
    Yea, my lord, I bid thee good-night.
    Forgive my disloyalty to thy will.

                                                                 (Exit Advisor)

Lord Jakob
    Do they not see the truth in the truth so alight?
    Do they not see my action already too late?
    Do they not see the fatherly duty that I must undertake,
    As lord and father alike?
    Well-meaning do I issue them to be,
    But e'en so can I not prove to be foolish.
    I do not take them as villains or mutineers,
    But they must see the sense in my actions.
    I thank heaven for my gift of allies fair,
    But I beg for fairness in judgement of my decrees.
    No lord can I act until I justice do,
    And 'til I protect my throne.
    I profess my past of foolery,
    To give leave to death and lunacy.
    Arise my men at arms, e'er true,
    Heaven calls us forth to our due.
    For our children and our descendants on,
    Shall we fore'er fight for a brighter dawn!

                                                                     (Exeunt)

ACT IV: Scene IV
(Setting: The library, where the Librarian is in sleep at his full desk.)

(Enter Professor)

Professor
    Awaken, book-keeper! Thy sources are asked!
    I have little time, and alike in patience.

Librarian
    Always be thee weary of those with little patience,
    For they are oft the first to anger and the first to blood.
    Yea, where can I prove of service?

Professor
    I am in need of the faceless tome,
    Hast thou it per usual?

Librarian
    I have it here, indeed.
    I find it odd nayless, high-teacher,
    Not e'en days ago in twain,
    Had I a boy come to ask for the same tome,
    That thou dost frequently bequest of me.
    Thou wouldst not proclaim to be spreading its message, indeed?

Professor
    I know not of whom thou speakest,
    But do not be so prying in business that is not thine.
    Nayless, what trouble would it be if I so had?
    Am I not charged to give my students wisdom?

Librarian
    Well indeed, my scholarly friend,
    But take it as so;
    When thou art to be taught, wouldst thou prefer to seek,
    Or be given that which thou hast wish to know?

Professor

The Apocalypse

>>To be given, of course.

Librarian
>>To be taught, very well. So therefore,
>>Thou wouldst seek that an instructor,
>>With either virtue or foul intent,
>>Tell his students his own interpretation and keep it so?
>>Not to let his instructed to interpret matters of themselves?

Professor
>>Is that not why we are called instructors?

Librarian
>>Very well, then now to this book.
>>In short, what canst thou tell me of it?

Professor
>>'Tis a book that speaks how the world is to end,
>>An end with the coming of time.
>>Eke how man can stop its coming.

Librarian
>>So be it. Now, if a curious student would come to thee,
>>To ask thee to teach yon message in lecture, wouldst thou do so?

Professor
>>Yea, without hesitation.

Librarian
>>And thy interpretation is fair to truth?

Professor
>>I pledge it to be so.

Librarian
>>So one man's view is truth?

Professor
>>Not fore'er so in all.

The Apocalypse

Librarian
> So each man's view alone holds truth?

Professor
> Ne'er so! There is wrong in many beliefs.

Librarian
> Very well, so wouldst thou then conclude thus:
> Truth is what mixes the views of the many?

Professor
> Mayhap 'tis so correct.

Librarian
> Very well. Now, thou hast said there is folly in many beliefs,
> Indeed?

Professor
> I spoke so directly.

Librarian
> Then what fact gives thy view truth?

Professor
> 'Tis my viewing from my reasoning.

Librarian
> And if the reasoning is tainted, would not the view be likewise?

Professor
> The logic so flows,
> So far would I concur, tome-master.

Librarian
> So then, in our reasoning we find fault,
> And there must one seek to examine.
> Let us then regard thy belief with this faceless tome.

Professor
> If thou wilt so regard,

The Apocalypse

    I agree to do so.

Librarian
    Thou art to say that this book tells of the end?
    The end of our world so fair in nature,
    But so foul with man?
    That is what thou dost grant?

Professor
    Yea, in simple measure I would say 'tis proper.
    But do not thou forget the nature of halting the end!

Librarian
    So the end is to come naturally,
    Or so from divine might of heaven?

Professor
    Both alike in dual power.

Librarian
    So thus the end will come?

Professor
    I had just so spoken.

Librarian
    And man has choice to stay this end?

Professor
    So he does, indeed.

Librarian
    And the end comes from nature and heaven?

Professor
    Yea, so as I spoke.
    What are these trifles of inquiries?

Librarian
    Patience, my friend, patience.

The Apocalypse

Thus, man hath power to rival heaven and nature?

Professor
    Nay, he doth not. Man is all too small and meek for such might.

Librarian
    My friend, bless thee,
    So how can he end the end if he cannot force nature?

Professor
    Because nature is not all-powerful.

Librarian
    So thou say that while man cannot force nature, he can force nature?

Professor
    In heaven's name, not at all!
    What absurdity is this?
    Nature is absent at times from whence man can dominate.

Librarian
    So what foretells that nature will be absent at the end,
    So to let man act?
    Would not nature be present when it brings the end?

Professor
    So would the end only come.

Librarian
    So man cannot force nature unless nature is absent?
    And man is to face nature, at the end of the worlds,
    When nature is present?
    That is what thou dost profess to say?

Professor
    The reasoning would so follow,
    But this is ridiculousness!
    We cannot know how nature works.

Librarian

The Apocalypse

    O, but thou hast spoken as one so certain!
    Nayless, I—as one of logic—will not say the tome is false.
    For as we spoke before, truth is not in one man,
    And if thou sayst this is thy interpretation,
    And thy interpretation is in flaw,
    That need not mean that the tome is false, merely thy reasoning.

Professor
    What insult! What lies!

Librarian
    Lies? Nay, my friend, the truth.

Professor
    O, so thou art now in truth?

Librarian
    Insofar as logic pure has lead me.
    And logic ne'er lies.

Professor
    And if thy logic is flawed?

Librarian
    As thine?
    Regardless, let us not degrade ourselves to insults,
    Let us turn once more to this book.

Professor
    What purpose hath that at all?
    Thou hast already expressed that thou seest no truth within it,
    Why wouldst thou care for it more?

Librarian
    I had ne'er spoken the book was false,
    Merely that thy reasoning was of flaw.
    The truth of the tome is still to question.

Professor
    So well, ask away thy questions,

>   This is of great tiring servitude to regard.

Librarian
>   Thus far have we then reasoned,
>   If thou so commend agreement.
>   We know that man cannot halt the end of the world,
>   Is it so?

Professor
>   I cannot agree, nay. But let us not tarry,
>   Continue with thy points.

Librarian
>   I did have need of thy acceptance,
>   But if thou dost not so elect I cannot act more,
>   For I cannot change thee.
>   Therefore regardless, my point required not thy point on that,
>   But more so for the great image of the end.
>   How do we know the end is at all to come?

Professor
>   I beg of thee to tell me if thou dost jest,
>   Art thou such a fool unreckoned by man?
>   Look skyward! The heavens have aligned,
>   Heaven speaks the story that the tome has forth put!

Librarian
>   So man has seen what heaven hath brought forth?

Professor
>   So had the book come about, for certain.

Librarian
>   And man wrote the tome thou so value?

Professor
>   I had spoken just that,
>   Dost thou not listen?

Librarian

The Apocalypse

    Peace, friend, peace.
    So if man hath written what he sees in heaven,
    Is there no chance that man hath seen falsely?

Professor
    What, was he a blind man,
    Who but assumed what was to lurk high above?

Librarian
    Nay, but did he not mayhap see the false message?

Professor
    What wretched falsehoods!
    Give but one moment of time,
    And think for that time given.
    Look thee at it thus;
    Man was curious and looked to heaven,
    And in the stars he saw the future to come.
    Yea, and in that tale of times to come,
    He alike saw the end of time.
    Thus, he acted to tell the revelation of his,
    And wrote so in a tome, as we now have.
    How could his word be wrong, if it from heaven came?

Librarian
    Dear, dear friend, what a fool thou canst be.
    For when man had spied heaven, it had just told its fate?
    Thus thou canst then believe so eagerly to what is not clear?
    No more words can we trade,
    That would not prove so empty?
    Yea, thou art truly lost, professor grand,
    And the tome only commands so.

Professor
    Foolish man! Think thee thyself all-knowing?
    The end will come, and so I state!
    Yet, I will not give so little hope,
    And serve to end the end of my being.
    The Apocalypse take the fools,
    I pledge myself to remain!

The Apocalypse

Librarian
> Now dost thou bring interest!
> What is of this Apocalypse?
> Dost thou not know what that word implies?

Professor
> Indeed, this is the uncovering, the revelation.

Librarian
> And what is this revelation?

Professor
> The revelation the prophet spoke in the knowing tome!
> The revelation there, and the revelation of the end.

Librarian
> But what dost thou know of this revelation?
> What dost thou know of the end?
> Could it not be the end of foolishness,
> And the revelation, one of wisdom?
> Why pledge for such a horrid end?

Professor
> The prophet hath so spoken, though man was he,
> That the end shall come.
> The story doth end thither, as our duel hither.

Librarian
> My friend, thou know'st not if the end shall come,
> No more than I if it shall not.
> But know that it need not all be so foul,
> When thy prophecy doth come by to us.
> Man can do nothing if that fate comes,
> But what is assured is this moment's life,
> Fret not on horrid and falsely stated prophecies,
> Live thy life, live merry and free.
> Work hard, toil much, and build thy legacy.

Professor

Talk! Thou knowest not, but I believe!
So is better than to fare empty-minded.
Live fair, but know thy limit,
The end will come and take them all,
As the end will come and spare us fair.
Now, I take my leave.
Good night and good fate,
Whate'er thou wilt see it to be.

(Exit Professor)

Librarian
    I know that I know nothing,
    Of the greater scheme of nature.
    I am man, and while man be great,
    He cannot always change his fate.
    Worry I shan't, and live fairly so,
    If the end doth come, so let it go.
    Fools art fools, as all men are,
    But hope they not the other scar.

(Exeunt)

ACT IV: Scene V
(Scene: The high balcony of justice, where Lord Jakob stands)

Lord Jakob
    O heaven, let thy bountiful blessings rain.
    Let thy spirits sing their songs of triumph.
    For in thy light and grace, beg I,
    With all exalted warmness and devotion,
    To have completed my quest.
    Let my city and all my people prosper.
    Let not rats and plague haunt our nights,
    And infest our days with worry and fear.
    Let not the beams and columns of our realm,
    Crumble from the tidings of madmen and traitors.
    Grant me my son, cursed by them though he may be,
    And let him return to my arms.
    Let him see the wrongs that he hath done,

And let justice be commanded upon him with virtuous fortune.
Yea, keep him from harm.
But of his masters, those vile fools and evil men,
Let justice burn them with righteous fire.
Let their cries ring to thy lofty domain,
And let all know what awaits a traitor in death.
'Tis no greater dishonour than a broken oath,
But alike no greater gift than a prudent head.
At last, mark I well the sight in memory,
Here come my great guards of might and wisdom!

(Enter Two Guards with Harald, Vilagre, Three Cultists, and Thief)

Hail, my soldiers of strong steel,
In blade and in courage!

First Guard
> Hail, our lord,
> Long life to thee!

Second Guard
> Hail, our lord,
> Honour to thy name!

Lord Jakob
> I spy thy bounty,
> Blessings to thee to act so well.
> But odd I see it,
> Where doth thy Captain stand?

First Guard
> Know we not, O lord,
> Shamed are we to say.

Second Guard
> Ere we left in our dual troop,
> Amongst our greater numbers of brothers,
> Our Captain gave us our vast commands,
> And sped away in great urgency.

The Apocalypse

Lord Jakob
>Naught of it,
>He shall come with time, I give it.
>But hark—Thy gifts do await thee!
>Ere we speak of thy villains wrested,
>Lay upon me thy tale of victory.
>How didst thou spy this modest number?
>This all that their order had in might?
>Where cam'st thou to find their shelter?

First Guard
>Wise were thou to act so swiftly, O lord.
>With ne'er our numbers great as thou spake,
>Our halt of this order may not have come.

Second Guard
>We, and our brothers of blades many,
>Had split to seek in the mother's womb,
>As thou hadst so commanded.

First Guard
>A troop of two had we all gone,
>As I and my brother here had done.
>One went to another; and another, another.
>Yea, and as we lurked amongst the slums,
>Between the shanties, and hiding thither,
>Spied we a door down to shadow.
>Marked with a flame burned upon its wood.
>We knew well what we had sought—

Second Guard
>So we descended, swords alight,
>Deeper and deeper in the hollowed passage.
>Not a breath was breathed,
>Nor a heart's thump beat,
>Ere we came upon a grotto, foul indeed.

First Guard
>Spacious, with walls of red stone, was it,
>Aglow from the pit of flames that held in centre.

The Apocalypse

> There all hooded, save the two not of yonder triple,
> Found we these cultists in great urgency.
> Little speech was passed, but great worry felt.
> Ere they could their escape then make,
> Stepped we from shadow with justice's call,
> And halted there the tidings of these traitors.

Second Guard

> Odd mayst thou also see, our lord,
> When we stepped from yon grotto door,
> Back to the light from horrid black,
> Spied we a thief, as thou canst spy here.
> With sly fingers he plucked the purse of an elder,
> But naught else could he steal ere we came upon him.

Lord Jakob

> Surely heaven hath blessed thee with justice,
> As thou art surely the true bringers of its deeds.
> Now wilt thou, in kind gesture,
> Show to me thy game well hunted?
> I spy the thief, in rags bears he his likeness,
> And eke my son Harald, though I cannot bear his sight.
> O my son, my youngest and most cherished,
> Why didst thou leave thy father's care?

Harald

> 'Twas thou who cast me from thy keep, O Jakob,
> Place not the blame to me ere thou look within thyself.

Lord Jakob

> Aye, well do I recall that dreadful, tempestuous night,
> And well do I regret my actions.
> Though I look to thee with greater lament, my son,
> To think thou mayst have killed thy dearest brother.

Harald

> Think not, know thee well that I did.

Lord Jakob

> O horrid rumour, wrought with truth!

What greater sin could a man profess?

First Guard
    My lord, with all duty and respect to thee,
    Ill fit are we to stand in thy private matters.

Second Guard
    Recall, that we have eke the masters that sullied thy son to sin.
    Seek justice to act upon them,
    And not to be foul to thy son,
    Who we shall keep in our minds impressed.

Lord Jakob
    Yea, fairly hast thou spoken, true friends.
    Indeed, so must we progress.
    Thus, let us disregard the common, and the once noble,
    And mark the futile desperate men,
    Seeking power they shall ne'er receive.

First Guard
    Indeed, my lord.

Second Guard
    If thou dost so command.

Lord Jakob
    Remove their shackles and let them stand before us,
    They shall not flee as long as we have steel at our sides.

First Guard
    By steel we save—

Second Guard
            Both lord and folk, indeed.

Lord Jakob
    So proceed we, mark well thou cowards.
    Thou hast slithered from my grip before, as e'er the evasive serpent.
    Now, at last, hast thou lost the game,
    Here to the raven of victory, of wisdom and power.

Thou hast taken my sons from virtue,
Slain one and corrupted another.
One can be redeemed with heaven's grace,
But one already sits in the high realm,
As due from thy poisoned blades of sorrow and despair.
Thy robes of black have e'er foul meaning,
Within my eyes of morality, full with tears.
But at last, thy pride shall be stripped from thee,
From thy crippled bodies of man-made monsters.
Guards! Tear from each their hoods,
Let their likeness befall my memory, and ne'er leave it hence.
Let me know who I shall execute with right,
Let heaven alike know who shall ne'er come to it.

First Guard
    So shall we!

Second Guard
    Heaven in sight, stand ready!

First Guard
    Mark! What great horror is this?
    'Tis he who whispers in the ears of our Lord Jakob!

First Cultist/Advisor
    Yea, so was I seen by mortal men.
    Amongst my fellows as brother!

Lord Jakob
    O raging blood, I thought of thee a friend!
    What madness must have befallen thee a kinsman to betray.
    My fury is e'er as great as before!

Second Guard
    Mark, shame to us eternal!
    'Tis our captain, commander of all our lord's men!

Second Cultist/Captain
    Yea, so was I hailed by mortal men.
    Amongst my order as enforcer!

First Guard
>Heaven, forgive us for serving a madmen and traitor!

Lord Jakob
>Nay, blame not thyself! This horrid traitor,
>Friend and ally thought I of him once alike,
>Protector of my kin and keep unto death,
>But wrong was I indeed.
>Fret not, my bravest knights of truth,
>Fore'er shalt thou be exempt of guilt and shame.
>Yea, we have still two more men to behold.

First Guard
>Behold! No greater shock here,
>When thou regard'st the mind's power.
>'Tis the professor, of the university.

Third Cultist/Professor
>Yea, so was I placed by mortal men.
>Amongst the order as teacher!

Second Guard
>Surely to poison our scholars' minds with his intent,
>To gain but more sheep to his serpent's order.

Lord Jakob
>Thou mayst slay me, thou mayst betray me,
>But ne'er could I fathom this act to poison the minds of youth!
>Truly must one be of such foul disposition to act so horridly.

First Guard
>And now awaits but one more man,
>What shock can still us befall?

Second Guard
>Is it the farmer, who poisons our food to eat?
>Is it the physician, who aids not our ailments?
>Mayhap is he a wizard, who casts our mind under spell?

The Apocalypse

First Guard
>So can we arise to answer,
>Tear off his hood, brother!

Second Guard
>What hold we here?
>Who may this man be, that memory does not recall?
>Toothless is he, and mad his eyes,
>Red with age and tiredness.
>Hairs out-fallen, pockmarked skin,
>E'er the sore to eyesight pure!

Vilagre
>Yea, so am I seen by mortal men.
>Known as Vilagre was I, in name.
>Yet amongst my order as leader!

Lord Jakob
>Yea, thy name befits thy character.
>Vilagre thou werest,
>Villain art thou now proclaimed.
>If thou art leader 'tis not well for thee,
>For greatest punishment will here be.
>Blades shall slash, and brands burn red,
>Hangman's rope and axe fall swift.
>Thou shalt feel the full fury of a father,
>So torn with rage and sorrow true.
>What hast thou to say?

Vilagre
>I know no fear, I am so leader.
>Let my brothers sing my praises,
>Was I not master of our order?

First Cultist/Advisor
>Leader art thou, Vilagre—

Second Cultist/Captain
>>But not of us.

Third Cultist/Professor
>Yea, Jakob, he was master.
>Not of us, but of action.
>He hath his fears, make no fault of it.
>But know, thy ills all spawn from he!

Vilagre
>Traitors! Brothers black with evil!
>Wilt thou see me glad in flames?
>With none my head atop my shoulders?
>With a rope round my neck to dangle from the rafters?

Lord Jakob
>Stop thy forked tongues, foul serpents,
>And alike thy venomous words.
>As none can see who is true leader—
>Or mayhap 'twas none, and all walked lonely—
>Shalt thou all feel the pain of justice.
>One of thee shall lose thy head,
>One of thee shall lose thy breath,
>One of thee shall lose thy arms,
>And one of thee shall lose thy will.

First Cultist/Advisor
>What of I?

Lord Jakob
>Thou shalt lose thy breath,
>For then canst thou not utter truthless words.

Second Cultist/Captain
>What of I?

Lord Jakob
>Thou shalt lose thy arms,
>For then canst thou not wield unjust blades.

Third Cultist/Professor
>What of I?

The Apocalypse

Lord Jakob
    Thou shalt lose thy head,
    For then canst thou not think thoughtless thoughts.

Vilagre
    What of I?

Lord Jakob
    Thou shalt lose thy will, O villain.
    I shall bring thee to the barren plains,
    Or to the highest mountains,
    And let Nature take her course with thee.
    For if thou art alone, thou hast nothing to lead.
    What dost thou think of these acts, my friends?

First Guard
    Wise are they indeed,
    And just to the act of which crimes they had done.

Second Guard
    Then the people shall know,
    To argue the lord is fair.
    But to act as foul as they,
    And steal his children in process,
    Is an act worth a coward's death.

First Guard
    No martyrs shall they be seen as,
    For if they were, great issue would we have.
    Bless thee to have acted so in haste, O lord,
    To not let their numbers have risen,
    And stopped their vile deeds at once.
    Heaven shall have thee renown!

Second Guard
    Amongst the people shalt thou be lord,
    To save the minds of men from madness.

Harald
    (Aside) Now, as these fools all quibble and mock,

The Apocalypse

    And grovel before the Lord Jakob,
    I shall make my leave in haste.
    If serpent alike am I to be,
    I shall thus slither in silence from this place,
    And retreat to reclaim that tome of mine.
    Those men, who once I called brothers,
    Are naught but cowards who abandon their goals,
    When faced with adversity.
    I know that truth shall be sought by me.
    I, who, while young may be, shall seek myself,
    To halt that end which these fools so forgot.
    I alone shall stand as victor.
    Look at Jakob, so proud of his deed,
    When he doth not know that ideas do not die with man.
    Mark his guards, as little children,
    Who praise and hail their lord,
    And thus call it fidelity.
    Fidelity! Where did that forgive?
    I stood along these men, held as brothers,
    But now who stand here in shame.
    Nay, 'tis not so, as I command.
    Let me flee, not as coward but as spirit!
    Farewell, O fools, flock to thyselves!

                                                   (Exit Harald)

Lord Jakob
    Yea, and if thou dost so proclaim,
    I then commend agreement.
    Let justice be acted upon these men.
    Though, let us consider the justice done,
    And its nature common.
    Shall we then punish this thieving man here?
    Is not his punishment, as alike his crime,
    Soothed by his presence here to horrid acts?
    Shall we not permit him life,
    And once this time, a haven of peace?
    Let him know, if thou wilt so confer,
    That I am not an old man of commons hereforth.
    I am strong to go with my deeds,

And all foul-doers shall receive their fate.
Yet, we see not here a common bandit often,
But a minor thief of new action.
Justice should be as justice deserves.
Let us act to these four, and leave this thief free.
Alike shall we need to make deed,
Within reason, and within compassion,
As I am yet father, as eternal,
Of my son Harald.
I will make speech with him,
But I will not be as weak as I had once been,
As he hath still done the sin of kin-slaying.

First Guard
    My lord, foolish have we been!
    Mark! Where hath thy son Harald gone?

Second Guard
    Indeed, so it is!
    What shall we in act do now?

Lord Jakob
    Fret not, my guards,
    He shall not have gone afar.
    Call the watchmen, close the gates;
    Let all await his likeness to travel.
    Do not worry with his presence,
    And let us regard these four to slay.
    Let the thief go; flee my friend,
    Go to light and go to virtue!
    Thou four! Let thy actions be remarked.
    My guards! Take thy action,
    Do as I shall have commanded,
    If thou dost recall,
    And seek to do righteousness for our citadel!

First Guard
    Yea, my lord, if thy wisdom doth so see.

Second Guard

The Apocalypse

> Arise, O lost and cowardly traitors,
> Let us go to meet our ends,
> If thou hast but little courage left,
> And have honour yet in mind.
> Time hath come to thee to meet thy destiny with pride,
> If thou art so foolish to keep thy beliefs.
> Hail to the lord, hail to justice!

First Cultist/Advisor
> Yea, so let us go forth to fate.

Second Cultist/Captain
> Shame to see us not in status great.

Third Cultist/Professor
> Come, brothers, together to fall.

Vilagre
> All as one, and in full, equal.

> > (Exit Guards, Cultists, Vilagre, and Thief)

Lord Jakob
> And so proceeds one foulness by another,
> With one succeeded, one new arisen.
> Nayless, thank heaven for duty,
> So far in righteousness imposed,
> And allow for hauntings to cure themselves through action.
> I regret nothing, and bless myself so.
> Through action of my own,
> And with my loyal guards,
> I have caused end to cults,
> And the orders of madmen.
> So, Above, let us go forth!
> So with heaven's grace, merrily thus bestowed,
> We sought out these orders that repentance owed.
> Seek out the lies and bless the truth,
> Give wisdom to man, and give him sooth.
> Unite the folk and work as one;
> The sun will hail us, and we, the sun!

(Exeunt)

ACT V: Scene I
(Scene: The library, with many piles of books)

(Enter Harald)

Harald
    Where art thou,
    Thou sacred tome of revelation?
    Grant me guidance in this tumultuous time,
    And bless me with long deceased wisdom.
    Where amongst the shadows and the light,
    Do we as mortals find what speaks truth?
    Naught, but thee, hath given such clarity,
    When all of life was but a mist.
    Thou cam'st to me, a blesséd fate was it for I,
    And gave life meaning.
    What of those who deny thy message?
    What of those who doubt devotion to thy cause?
    Let those faithful rejoice in harmony,
    When the end comes and wreaks panic on the sheep.
    Those of us who know, few we may be,
    Shall stay in peace to know our ability.
    But those who mock and jeer with naught of respect,
    What can we do but silence their utterings?
    Little peace have we already, less do we need,
    So tidings go, and so shall they stay.
    Ho, who goes to whisper in the dark,
    Pray give thy image shape in light!

(Enter Librarian)

Librarian
    I gamble it to be odd, my youth,
    That thou art alone to speak of light,
    With yon a heart so blackened with strife,
    And with words so foul of villains, pierced.
    Well know I those robes of raven's black,

The Apocalypse

        And quick does word spread amongst the populous.
        Thou art Harald, youngest son of Jakob.
        Slayer of thy brother, in accordance to an order,
        An order so devoted to what thou dost speak.
        Am I false in all my tellings?

Harald
        Bookkeeper! I seek my tome,
        The tome—

Librarian
                The tome, I profess, of the end of our world?

Harald
        Yea, alike the same,
        How didst thou know?

Librarian
        I had spoken with the Professor of the university, who,
        As thou wilt now know, belonged to thy order.
        Not e'en a day's length hence,
        We in twain had recalled the tome,
        And debated its factuality.

Harald
        Yea, so does one make sense of fact.
        What end didst thou reach in talk?
        Hast thou taken the book's message in thought?
        What is thy impression here now?

Librarian
        Why dost thou fret so great for my impression, young one?

Harald
        Thou dost seem like great a man,
        Wisdom in thy eyes, and knowledge in thy image.
        Those I regarded as brothers in my past,
        Hath shown themselves to be naught but cowards;
        Easy to falter, quick to surrender.

Librarian
>To hear the story of one man over thy own?
>'Tis not a mark of cowardice, I grant.
>I pledge I will not hold back here more,
>Though I believe thou wilt not enjoy my words,
>And hold thine still in high regard.

Harald
>Nay, for so I profess that I crave to know,
>For I do not see this as cowardice.

Librarian
>So be it, I shall then repeat my claims,
>As I had to this past Professor.
>Thou dost confess to see the end of worlds, indeed?
>How it shall, is mystery, but the end general, 'tis certain?

Harald
>Yea, the end shall come as I do see.

Librarian
>And what see we as worlds?

Harald
>How dost thou mean?

Librarian
>Do we speak of the world entire?
>Do we speak of a world afar?
>Do we speak of empires once of great repute?
>Do we speak of lands far and separate from ours?
>Thus do I intend to speak.

Harald
>I confess I do not know.
>I presumed the world as so was stated.

Librarian
>Be wary of words so plainly uttered,
>As so do prophets oft disguise their words.

> Now, we confess to not know these worlds,
> Speak we not of ere-fallen worlds and empires?
> Have these not been of vast lands,
> Only to fall one day and leave history be?
> Is not every man's life his own world,
> And shall this not alike one day end?
> How can we seek the value true of these words?

Harald
> Moreover, I do not know foremore!

Librarian
> Precise in thought!
> Then let us continue.
> If the end was to come,
> What wouldst thou do?

Harald
> I would stop its power, if I was so able.
> And how may that be, thou mayst ask,
> But that lies in the matter of virtue.
> Heaven would give those of faith to life,
> And those without, to death.

Librarian
> Let us then ask, my youth,
> Is nature in heaven's power?

Harald
> So it is, by heaven's command.
> E'en so if heaven was in nature's power.

Librarian
> Very well. Now, can man halt nature's will?
> Can man pierce a fierce wind with a sword,
> Or hold his hand against a flood?

Harald
> No, so can he not,
> It is not in his ability.

Librarian
> And would nature destroy the world as of heaven's demands?

Harald
> Yea, so it would.

Librarian
> And I gamble with fires, and floods, and such?

Harald
> Yea, so is foretold.

Librarian
> And could man halt such things?

Harald
> Nay—
> I pledge he could not.

Librarian
> Thus, we know that we do not know the nature,
> Of which the end shall come,
> Nor if it shall come at all.
> But e'en if it does, we cannot halt it;
> So is it as we have reasoned?

Harald
> Yes, I confess with heavy heart that it so seems,
> Thou art causing fear in me, book-keeper.

Librarian
> So is well, for fear shall oft bring about reason,
> If so it permits.
> Now, thou speakest of the end,
> But think thee not that this tome may cause the end itself?
> Those who did not believe shall cause panic,
> Whilst those of faith shall not;
> Leaving men to men, and with his fear bring his own end?
> Is not so the nature of men?

The Apocalypse

Harald
  From observation 'tis so seeming.

Librarian
  My youthful boy,
  Dost thou not see that this end is but the end of life,
  The end that comes to all?
  This Apocalypse thou seest,
  This Revelation of ends,
  'Tis not some doomsday prophecy,
  'Tis to tell man of his mortality.
  Thy end may come in flood or fire all,
  Man must learn that he is mortal,
  And let so, oft seek the path of godhood.
  Death is human, and shall tell us when we have ended.
  This may seem as the end of worlds,
  But the good life fears no death,
  For he knows he hath done good and left his story to tell onward.
  This is yon revelation that man must know.
  The end shall certain come,
  As it does for all,
  Yet it shall not end our worlds as thou hast thought.
  Fear not, my boy, live thy life,
  Fare well and prosper, then wilt thou be immortal!

Harald
  Dost thou tell me, book-keeper friend,
  That I had slain my brother for natural course?
  That I had brought for him the end early,
  Lost to no legacy, little to memory?
  Lost time and ability, as due to a fool's hand?
  Have I given my father grief,
  For irrational vision of fact,
  To pervert and warp to a lie?
  My hands! They have blood upon them!
  I am a murderer, kin-slayer,
  Greatest sinner and foulest boy!
  Heaven curse me for eternity!

Librarian
> Peace, my child, peace to thee.
> Seek virtue in horror—

Harald
> Nay, 'tis not so possible, friend!
> Dost thou not see what villainy I have done?
> I have torn my family apart in tatters,
> Worse above all, I have killed.
> At so young an age as mine, not of warfare,
> Nor of defence *for* my kin.
> Nay! So *to* my kin!
> Leave thy blessings, I am not worthy,
> I have no gift but death to await!

(Exit Harald)

Librarian
> So hath it been to come and pass,
> As so runs destiny and fate so often.
> Though I beg the boy did not seek as he spoke,
> To wish death when so early in life.
> Let father accept son once more,
> Let there be tranquillity, and no more war.
> Let those ashamed with guilt,
> With given peace, be given what they wilt.
> Do not let dwell what must be left,
> Let speech and negotiation be deft!

(Exeunt)

ACT V: Scene II
(Scene: The Lord Jakob's study)

(Enter First Guard and Lord Jakob)

Lord Jakob
> Hast thou spied to all thou couldst?

First Guard

As much as skill will permit, my lord.

Lord Jakob
And the villains of that black order,
Hath justice been done upon them?

First Guard
One breath, and one head,
One of arms, and one will to lose.
All as thou hast commanded, O lord.
Our fellows go now as we speak,
To leave the leader of the order in his solitude.
High off in the mountains have they departed.
But what now of thy son?

Lord Jakob
I know not, but I pledge he shall soon come,
Or so can I hope dearly.
Keep yet the watchman's eyes agape,
All sight is still needed,
And so be heeded.
If thou couldst, my friend and ally,
Couldst thou leave me in a moment's peace?
I require time to ponder of matters,
What shall I do, what shall I say?
Those matters small, but of great material.

First Guard
Certainly, my lord, thou needst but ask.
Stay in peace, worry thyself not too great.
Peace shall be found at last,
Here in thy domain.

Lord Jakob
So can I hope.

First Guard
So can I pledge true.

(Exit First Guard)

Lord Jakob
>And hither I am left alone,
>To wonder of my actions,
>To wonder of my sons.
>Doth one still me despise?
>Doth the other sleep e'er peaceful?
>Have I made just action to punish the foul,
>Or was I as foul as those I had punished?
>I pray I shall know with time.
>But one matter doth still vex my conscience,
>Should I encage my son, so seeking freedom of mind?
>I pledge he hath lost himself certain,
>But how would I proceed if I had him?
>Would he not wish to be gone of me?
>Should I leave him to fare alone,
>To do as he sees fair?
>Nay, he is still of such youth,
>Could he not be taught the right again?
>So shall time foretell, I hope.

(Enter Harald)

Harald
>Greetings, O father mine.

Lord Jakob
>Art thou a spectre?
>Hast thou passed and come to haunt me?

Harald
>Nay, Father, 'tis not so.
>I have seen the wrongs of my mind,
>And have come to confess my shame and slavish guilt.

Lord Jakob
>O my son, sense hath come to thee at last.
>Wilt thou not come to be blessed e'er more?

Harald

Nay! For such do I not deserve, my father!
I have done horrid crimes;
'Tis not a rumour that I was one my brother's murderers,
And the blade I wielded pierced my brother.
I deserve no blessings,
Save only the blessing of death.
So must it be.

Lord Jakob

My son, my son,
How couldst thou do this?
Hadst thou no love for thy kin?

Harald

Do not speak so!
I feel what I have done,
I shame myself eternal to have done so,
But the sands of time have fallen,
And naught may raise them e'er again.
Thus, must we seek what I deserve.
I speak exclusive of my punishment,
And naught else that I so less deserve.

Lord Jakob

Nay, my son, let me embrace thee nayless.

Harald

I cannot permit it so, Father,
Such love would foolishly make me see no shame.
Love would not be fit to befall me,
As I deserve not its warmth and purity.
Heaven curse me eternal for my actions;
I will cry and cry unto death,
And past death will I cry further,
So for all eternity.
Forgive me, Father, if thou couldst,
I shall go to burn, whilst my brother sleeps.
Heaven, curse me onward!

(Exit Harald)

Lord Jakob
>   Nay, my son, halt one moment!
>   Where canst thou go?
>   Where wilt thou go?
>   Give thyself peace, thou werest lost afore!
>   Heaven forgive my youngest child,
>   Do not let him be hated, but upon be smiled!
>   Let not he do foolish act,
>   So as to harm himself without tact.
>   Seek him out must I, and grant him peace,
>   Ere the tidings come to horrid cease.

(Exeunt)

ACT V: Scene III
(Scene: The temple, where the priest arranges at the altar)

(Enter Harald)

Harald
>   Heaven-speaker!
>   Temple-master!
>   I seek thy assistance anon!
>   Wilt thou not bear my trifles?
>   Cure my soul, ere I cause it failure?
>   Wilt thou not speak to heaven for me,
>   As my voice is mute to its ears?
>   Cannot my soul be redeemed,
>   Though my doubts are to its value?
>   Pledge to answer truthfully,
>   Give me notice of my worth to the above!

Priest
>   Peace, young one, rest thy lungs held in fear.
>   Speak to me as one that is coy,
>   Let whispers be uttered in this house.
>   Tell me, what so plagues thy spirit?

Harald

The Apocalypse

    O spirit-man, dost thou not mark my image?
    I am the Lord Jakob's youngest son Harald;
    Mayhap hast thou heard of my shame?
    As I have been a part an order of mindless zealotry,
    And thus have shamed my father and our family.

Priest

    Nay, I have not so heard.
    'Tis better to leave out words of rumour,
    For they are oft to smear the names of the good.
    But what is now to worry thee, my boy?
    Hast thou not forsaken these madmen,
    Then returned to thy father?

Harald

    'Tis not so light, I grant it,
    I had not purely joined to seek which was but nature's path,
    I had done horror upon the non-believers as well.
    I had further, in foolish disposition,
    And of weakened mind, no less,
    Moved to act and slay my brother,
    Who stood adamant against this foul order of insanity.
    Thus he paid the greatest bounty of his,
    As a heretic, in the eyes of such these madmen,
    And one of their number was I.
    I feel naught but sorrow,
    I abhor my existence,
    I seek naught but an end to my horrid character.
    I beg of heaven to curse me,
    But more I beg to the high ones,
    To see my brother in his rest,
    To hear my fate from him,
    To hear the suffered give verdict to the torturer.
    I cannot bear it longer. Temple-keeper,
    Tell me, for heaven doth not come for me longer.
    As I have done the most heinous of deeds,
    The slaying of a brother, of a kinsman.
    Wilt thou not tell to me what I could do?

Priest

The Apocalypse

    Fates forgive me, whate'er can I say?
    I am terrified young one, aghast of thy behaviour,
    But know this; destiny will open to thee,
    As long as fidelity still stays within thee.
    Thou carest for thy brother,
    Thou lament his early end,
    Thou abhor thyself for thy actions, as any man would.
    Let not thy past taint thy present,
    Let not fate make thee fear the future.
    Act my boy; prayer shall not help thee great,
    Thou must act to show amends,
    Again to show to thy brother thy thoughts,
    Not to the heavens.

Harald
    Is not heaven the truest of sources?

Priest
    Nay, that lurks within man,
    And so it shall stay eternal.
    Thank the fates for what thou hast,
    But look within thyself for what thou hast not.
    E'en more, if thou wilt hear my words,
    Think not thy past self as thy true form.
    That piece, thither we see it now,
    Had died when thou didst act so foul.
    But thy purest sense, thy true and good self,
    That is what thou needst find.
    Seek thy destiny, but with hearings to thy brother's spirit.

Harald
    Yea, fate-seeker, bless thee. In fate's name, so shall I do.
    For now do I see what must be done.
    Let heaven spy me, after Andreas hath.
    Let his spirit look to me as brother,
    If heaven hath granted him forgiveness.
    Bless thee all, now I act!
    Once I was lost, now am I not.
    Let the old self of mine die and rot.
    Hear, my brother, slain by me,

The Apocalypse

Do let us e'er brothers be!
I come to thee with but one way,
Ere comes the final end of day!

(Exit Harald)

(Exeunt)

ACT V: Scene IV
(Scene: The city square, where Three Civilians walk the market)

(Enter Lord Jakob and Two Guards)

Lord Jakob
    Keep thy eyes alight,
    Spy my son if thou canst,
    Where'er in this crowd he may lurk.

First Guard
    So shall we do, our lord.

Second Guard
    But think thee that he would stay amongst here in number?

Lord Jakob
    I profess I know not where he may be,
    Amongst the many that he be not spied so simply,
    Or in the recluse of the lonesome alley of cobbled streets.

First Guard
    But question thee not that he may have the citadel departed?

Second Guard
    In shame to become a hermit,
    Off in the far reaches of solitude mayhap?

Lord Jakob
    Nay, my friends, he did not so declare.
    Would he have wished it so he would have told to me,
    Though plead I do not seek for him,

The Apocalypse

    In self, or with great armies to search.

First Guard
    And if heaven would so allow?

Lord Jakob
    Heaven doth not declare what men shall do,
    Nor is it privy to that which men do not others tell.

Second Guard
    But yet it seems the daunting task to spy him in sight,
    Amongst these greater numbers.

Lord Jakob
    We shall search, and thus shall see,
    But search we must indeed.

                                        (Enter Harald)

First Civilian
    Hark! Look there!

Second Civilian
        'Tis a man atop the tower.

Third Civilian
                What lurks he there?

First Guard
    My lord, spy that image atop the tower!
    'Tis Harald! What shall we do?

Second Guard
    My lord, what seeks he there?

Lord Jakob
    Silence, he speaks!
    Pray listen now, to act anon.

Harald

The Apocalypse

Ho, O people of the citadel!
I am Harald, son of thy Lord Jakob.
Know thee not that I be mortal?
Art thou aware of what horrors I have done, before heaven,
In a maddened mind?
Pray thou ne'er know if thou dost not,
And e'en for those who do,
Forgive me for what foulness I have committed.
Yea, for I, when still in bonds of madness,
Thought fit to put mine brother, Andreas,
Heir was he to this great citadel,
To death, for holding opposed belief to my order past.
Ere 'twas known to me,
Thought I this vibrant world of ours to perish,
In great storm of fire and large waves of a doomsday.
Withal my insane conceptions I faced to act for others,
Others laden with inept theory,
And alike with encaged fury of long held sufferings.
Those desperate to seek meaning ideal to their black lies.
I was once one of these fools,
And thus in action, had done the act so egregious,
So foul and horrid, to slay my kin in coldest bloodshed.
Be not as I, so flexible to appeal to any fool,
To become a fool in thy own right.
I pledge I did the most cruelty I could do,
But mark! I am not yet guiltless.
E'er-hating of my heinous actions,
And ne'er forgivable in the eyes of man.
It shall not be plain to say, that with time to pass,
The tale of Harald will be one of example,
To tell to the young what lengths a man can go,
If so seduced by his own stupidity.
Who can deny the yearnings of a man's heart?
But there's difference between yearning,
And that nature of mindlessness.
My crimes of evil shall haunt for eternity,
Until the end, and the end thereafter,
Upon Earth and within the realms of man.
So fret not, thou good folk,
Thy crimes are not as great as mine!

The Apocalypse

Know thee how it feels to lose thyself?
To cry at thy wanton firmament,
And thence to have no voice with which to scream?
To beg for forgiveness, but to know thou shan't receive it?
My actions were not my own,
But I was in action there,
And was one to hold close to my victim, my brother.
I curse myself, without the aid of gods and men.
Yea, men! Indeed, they as well.
Was I not alike any soul,
Blessed to live amongst men,
And alike to be damned?
'Tis naught but a bounty,
A burden much to bear, to lurk with men,
A beast so cruel, as I, to act.
This nature so abhorrent,
This damned and cursed petrifice,
To grasp the senses, and make one act alike another.
To seek the acceptance of those adept with thee,
Those men too stubborn to see the good in others,
If they have but any within themselves.
Love thy kin, O people,
Love thy fellow man within thy given reason,
And live not as I once had.
To despise those opposed to thee, without logic.
To slay my kin with wanton and devilish eagerness,
Not akin to e'en the blackest of demons.
I seek no forgiveness from myself,
For I know I shall none receive.
I seek only forgiveness from my brother,
His spirit entered in the halls of gods.
I seek only the passing agreement of fate,
To know I have but little good within me still.
I seek no life onward, for I am not worthy.
I wish not for mundane punishment,
For not a measly penance can be torturous to wrong my shame,
And give sufficient sentence.
Let myself go by Nature's forces,
By my own will to be thrown,
With courage and with dignity,

The Apocalypse

>   To make the election thus.
>   'Tis with this I throw myself,
>   Beyond the grasps of men and his steel.
>   My likeness here to fall,
>   Dare I afflict thee all this vision?
>   Fare well to all, fare well at last,
>   Heaven above, hear once my plea!
>   O, beloved Andreas, all love to thee!

Lord Jakob
>   His likeness falls,
>   He hath cast himself from atop the tower!

First Guard
>   My lord, nay!
>   See not this horror!

Second Guard
>   Cover thy eyes,
>   In affections, I plead!

Lord Jakob
>   Yea, I cannot look to it.

First Guard
>   'Tis done. O, cruel fates be played,
>   What rueful turn is this?
>   Could not such misery be halted?

Second Guard
>   O our lord, weep not,
>   We beg of thee earnestly.
>   Too great the burden 'tis to see,
>   To see fair Harald far afallen,
>   And thee, once so strong, to weep.

Lord Jakob
>   O horror, O sullen tragedy,
>   Here hath my misery on me befallen.
>   Agape in black prudence lies my heart,

The Apocalypse

      As does my youngest child at the foot of the tower.
      My beloved, tortured once alike by misery,
      And so elected not to be, as Harald had.
      Thus passed her son a likewise deed,
      And passed from me all too quickly.
      My beloved, and two our gifts,
      Have from my grasps been stolen.
      I beg of thee, O wicked heavens,
      Take no more, as I give all:
      My crown, my lands, myself indeed.
      Let no father be like as I,
      Ere he lets all he loves to die.
      Let those ancient ways of yore,
      Last for eternity e'ermore.
      The devil, the devil, lies within men,
      But eke in the hearts of gods again!

Narrator
      Erewhile had we all thought our words true,
      But do we know what we truly thought we knew?
      Is all we hear of same equal worth,
      Or is there anywhere whence truth gives birth?
      Nary a man would so swear his word,
      Ifsoever he knew men thusly concurred.

                                                    (Exeunt)

FINIS

www.ingramcontent.com/pod-product-compliance
Lightning Source LLC
Chambersburg PA
CBHW032007080426
42735CB00007B/538